Critical Thinking
for AS Level

More related titles

Critical Thinking for Students
Learn the skills of critical assessment and effective argument

'A really useful introduction to developing and improving a core skill.'
– Association of Commonwealth Universities Bulletin

How to Pass Exams Every Time
*Proven techniques for any exam that will boost your confidence and
guarantee success*

'If you want a book that is excellently written and will show you how to study and approach
exams, buy this!' – Amazon reviewer

Writing an Essay
Simple techniques to transform your coursework and examinations

'There is a lot of good sense in this book.' – Times Educational Supplement

howtobooks
Send for a free copy of the latest catalogue to:
How To Books
3 Newtec Place, Magdalen Road,
Oxford OX4 1RE, United Kingdom
email: info@howtobooks.co.uk
http://www.howtobooks.co.uk

Critical Thinking
for AS Level

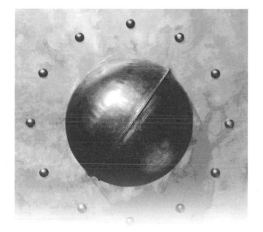

Roy van den Brink-Budgen

howtobooks

Published by How To Books Ltd,
3 Newtec Place, Magdalen Road,
Oxford, OX4 1RE, United Kingdom
Tel: (01865) 793806 Fax: (01865) 248780
email: info@howtobooks.co.uk
http://www.howtobooks.co.uk

Text © Roy van den Brink-Budgen 2005

First edition 2005
Reprinted 2005

British Library Cataloguing in Publication Data
A catalogue record for this book is available from
the British Library.

Produced for How To Books by Deer Park Productions, Tavistock
Typeset by *specialist* publishing services ltd, Milton Keynes
Cover design by Baseline Arts Ltd, Oxford
Printed and bound by Bell & Bain Ltd, Glasgow

Note: The material contained in this book is set out in good
faith for general guidance and no liability can be accepted
for loss or expense incurred as a result of relying in particular
circumstances on statements made in the book. The laws and
regulations are complex and liable to change, and readers should
check the current position with the relevant authorities before
making personal arrangements.

CONTENTS

Tomorrow.

PREFACE   ix

1 ARGUMENTS   1

What are arguments in Critical Thinking?   1

- What is an argument?   1
- Activity 1   3

Arguments and explanations   5

What forms can arguments take?   6

- Simple forms of argument   6
- Activity 2   7

Simple forms of argument with more than one reason   7

- Activity 3   9

The Nature of Conclusions   9

- Finding conclusions   10
- Drawing conclusions   11
- Drawing intermediate conclusions   12

Activity 1: commentary   16

Activity 2: commentary   17

Activity 3: commentary   18

2 CREDIBILITY OF EVIDENCE   **19**

Why is credibility an issue in Critical Thinking?   19

Credibility of reports   20

- How context can affect credibility   22
- Issues of perception, language, interpretation, and judgement   27

Credibility of evidence   28

- Eye-witness accounts   28
- Reporting   29
- Reporting of reporting   30
- Other sources of data   32

Credibility and bias   34

- Accidental bias   34
- Deliberate bias   35

Judging credibility: possible weaknesses   36

- Vested interest   36

Judging credibility: possible strengths   38

- Neutrality   38
- Expertise   40
- Ability to perceive   43

Judging credibility: both strengths and weaknesses   43

- Motive   43
- Reputation   44

Judging a case   46

- Corroboration   46
- Conflict   47
- Identifying sides   48
- Looking for the weight of evidence   49
- Doing the credibility calculus: evaluating the quality of each side   49
- Making a judgement   52

3 ASSUMPTIONS   **53**

Assumptions explained   53

Finding assumptions   55

- The negative test   56
- Activity 4   58

Thre.

Assumptions and the evaluation of arguments 59

• Activity 5 62

Activity 4: commentary 63

Activity 5: commentary 65

4 EVIDENCE **67**

Asking questions about evidence used in arguments 67

Different types of statistics 70

• Percentages 71

• Numbers 72

• Rates 74

• Indices 76

• Timescales 77

• Using unusually-presented evidence 79

Generalising from evidence 80

• Activity 6 83

• Activity 7 84

Activity 6: commentary 85

Activity 7: commentary 89

5 EVALUATING ARGUMENTS **91**

Looking for strengths in arguments 91

Looking for weaknesses in arguments 93

• *Post hoc* 94

• Straw Man 97

• *Ad hominem* 99

• *Tu quoque* 100

• Circular arguments 102

• Slippery slopes 102

• Restricting the options 103

• Making irrelevant appeals 104

    Appeal to popularity 104

    Appeal to authority 106

    Appeal to pity 107

fri

Sub

6 SPECIAL KINDS OF ARGUMENT CONTENT   **109**

Analogies   109

• Activity 8   113

Counter-arguments   113

Definitions   116

Principles   118

• Activity 9   120

Hypothetical arguments   120

Necessary and sufficient conditions   123

Activity 8: commentary   124

Activity 9: commentary   128

7 PRODUCING ARGUMENTS   **129**

Producing a reason against the author's conclusion   130

Producing evidence in support of reasons   131

• Hypothetical evidence   131

• Everyday evidence   132

Producing a reason for the author's conclusion   132

Producing two reasons against the author's conclusion   133

Producing two reasons for the author's conclusion   135

Drawing intermediate conclusions   136

Including counter-arguments   139

PREFACE

This book has one aim. This is to take you through all you need to learn in order to succeed in the AS examination in Critical Thinking. It does this by explaining all the skills that you need to have, and by giving you examples and exercises to help you practise them.

The book won't feature smiling wizards pointing at things you should take note of. You don't need them. It won't feature images of light bulbs being lit up when something significant is being looked at. It's enough that your brain lights up. And we hope it will. It won't give you lists of 'handy hints' (such as 'remember to take a pen with you into the exam room' or 'eat a banana before the exam') because this is a book that wants to get you excited about Critical Thinking, not to insult you as if you can't think.

Critical Thinking is indeed a very exciting subject. Part of its excitement is that you can see the world differently once you've been doing it. It is very much hoped, then, that reading this book will have that effect. It's different from so many other subjects, in that it teaches you skills. Just like swimming, driving, skiing, dancing, and anything else that requires skills, once you can do it you feel different. You feel good, in control, on top of it, competent, special.

Over many years, I have taught Critical Thinking to hundreds of students throughout the country (including, for some years, young men in prison). This experience has very much helped me in the writing of this book. I am aware, for example, of those areas of the subject that students say they find difficulty with and I have, hopefully, made them less difficult. I am also aware of the point that, though Critical Thinking has value in so many different ways, students are often taught it as if it just applies to reading something like *The Independent* or worrying about big issues like euthanasia. We need to see that it applies pretty well everywhere. When a cosmetic company claims that they have proved that a skin cream reduces wrinkles (by, in small print, at the bottom of the TV screen, showing that it was tested on 50 women over three weeks, 68 per cent of whom agreed that it did), then we switch on our Critical Thinking. When our favourite football (or cricket) team plays, we apply our Critical Thinking to reports of why they lost (or won).

So, though you're not going to find little boxes with handy tips inside, there are two obvious handy tips that I want to pass on. Read this book. Practise your skills on whatever material you find: the sports pages, adverts, articles about diets in glossy magazines, whatever. Then you should do well.

Roy van den Brink-Budgen
September 2005

To Annie, for every reason.

ARGUMENTS

WHAT ARE ARGUMENTS IN CRITICAL THINKING?

WHAT IS AN ARGUMENT?

The word 'argument' is not one that is used only in Critical Thinking. In general use, the word has a number of possible meanings. These are some of them:

conflict of views   debate
dialogue   discussion
dispute   exchange of views
questioning

Though these meanings don't necessarily capture exactly what is meant by the term **argument** in Critical Thinking, all of them contain some of the features of this term.

- **Conflict of views** and **exchange of views** highlight differences in positions that are being defended.

- **Debate** suggests the process of defending and attacking positions (as could **discussion**).

- **Dialogue** is very open-ended, in that the dialogue could be about anything (catching up with news, exchanging information), but it could be in the form of an argument.

- **Dispute** suggests a difference between at least two positions.

- **Questioning** can suggest many things, some of which have nothing to do with argument ('what would you like to eat?'), but it can also include the meaning of asking questions in order to clarify or extend an argument ('what can this evidence mean?').

Arguments in Critical Thinking are in some ways like all the meanings listed on page 1, but there are features that make them distinct. To highlight these special features, consider the following:

> *'I think that football players get paid far too much money.'*
> *'Why do you think that?'*
> *'Because it's my opinion that they do.'*

Has an argument been presented? Is there an argument going on? Is giving an opinion the same as giving an argument? Looking at our previous list of words, we could say that there has been a **dialogue** (two people are talking) and there has been some **questioning**. But there hasn't yet been what we are looking for in a Critical Thinking *argument*. Just giving an opinion is not the same thing. What happens if the dialogue continues?

> *'Do all football players get paid too much?'*
> *'Those in the Premiership certainly do.'*
> *'I don't agree.'*

Is there now an argument? There is certainly more dialogue and questioning. So we are now a little clearer as to what is meant. And we have a clear expression of disagreement (a 'conflict of views' and 'dispute').

But, as yet, Critical Thinkers have not found an argument. One person has expressed an opinion and the other has expressed their disagreement with it. So, let's turn the conversation towards an argument.

> *'Players in the Premiership shouldn't get so much money because there aren't that many clubs that can afford those sort of salaries.'*

At last, the Critical Thinker has an argument! The word 'because' is crucial. The argument can be presented in the following way:

> *There aren't that many football clubs that can afford to pay really high salaries to their players. So footballers in the Premiership get paid too much.*

Though, in one way, you could say that an opinion is being given just like before, more is going on. A reason has been given why footballers are paid too much.

Thus we can now see that an argument in Critical Thinking is more than just expressing an opinion. There has to be some sort of support (however thin) for the position that's being argued for.

ACTIVITY 1

Which of the following dialogues contains an argument?

(1) 'Everyone is so selfish these days.'

'Surely you can't say that.'

'Why not? It's what I think.'

(2) 'I think that *Coronation Street* is the best soap on TV.'

'But what about *Eastenders*?'

'*Coronation Street* is much better than *Eastenders*.'

(3) 'Dogs are much less suitable than cats as pets for old people. They need walking every day.'

'I agree with you.'

(4) 'Volvos are safe and reliable cars.'

'But aren't they expensive?'

'Not compared to other safe and reliable cars.'

(5) 'Vegetarians tend to be healthier and live longer than people who eat meat.'

'That's why I'm a vegetarian.'

'And that's why other people should be too.'

(6) 'It would be a good idea if people could carry on working beyond the normal retirement age.'

'I don't think that they should be allowed to.'

'But if they can't, then the country won't be able to afford to pay for their pensions.'

Doing Activity 1 will have shown you that an argument must be more than the undeveloped expression of a fact, opinion, or whatever. There must be something more: it must go somewhere. It must use the fact, opinion, or whatever to argue *for* or *that* something. Of course, this is not to say that where the argument has gone is still not, in the end, someone's opinion. But the mere expression of a statement as opinion needs to be distinguished from a developed statement as opinion.

It's wrong to catch fish.

Here there is no more than an expression of opinion. It doesn't go anywhere. It is not an argument. You could respond by saying 'That's just your opinion'.

Fish can feel pain. So it's wrong to catch them.

In this example, though the author of the argument is making the same point, they have now added something to make their point more than just undeveloped opinion. If you disagree with their (developed) opinion, they have given you a very different task in responding to it. You can't get away with saying 'It's just your opinion that it's wrong to catch fish'. You've now got to deal with their point about fish feeling pain.

Activity 1 used examples of dialogues. But most arguments that we come across are not dialogues. We don't have to be talking to someone else to produce an argument.

Though they are highly skilled at what they do, footballers in the Premiership get paid far more money than other similarly skilled sportspeople, such as cricketers, rugby players, and swimmers. These footballers shouldn't get paid as much as they do.

Here there is nobody disagreeing with the person who's putting the argument forward, but you will see that an argument has still been made. (Premiership footballers get paid far more money than other similarly skilled sportspeople. Therefore they shouldn't get paid as much as they do.)

What Activity 1 will also have shown you is that arguments can include all the things on our list of possible meanings. But, very importantly, arguments need not include any of them.

Olympic athletes are amongst the best in the world. So young people who want to represent their country in the Olympics need to practise their sport.

This argument is probably one that everyone would agree with. Thus there is no conflict or exchange of views; there is no debate, discussion, or dispute; there is no questioning; there is no dialogue. But it is an argument. The author of it goes somewhere. They take the statement about Olympic athletes and they build something on it.

One of the features of arguments is that they are designed to be *persuasive*. The person putting the argument forward wants us to accept something (it's wrong to catch fish; young people who want to be Olympic athletes need to practise). This is not to say that the argument *will* be persuasive, but that the person making it intends it to be so.

You can see that the plain statement 'It's wrong to catch fish' is less persuasive than the argument 'Fish can feel pain. So it's wrong to catch them'. The greater potential for someone being persuaded in the second version comes from the fact that a reason is given why it's wrong to catch fish.

ARGUMENTS AND EXPLANATIONS

In an argument, we look to see what we are supposed to be persuaded of.

Fish can feel pain. So it's wrong to catch them.

The author, it will be remembered, wants us to accept that it's wrong to catch fish. Put more strongly, that it's true that it's wrong to catch fish. However, when we look at explanations, the intention of their author is not to try to persuade us that something is true.

The car hasn't had a service for two years. It often doesn't start in the morning.

In this example, there is an attempt to link the two statements such that the first is the possible explanation for the second. But the author isn't trying to persuade us that the car doesn't often start in the morning. That's taken as a given fact. Consider the difference in the next example.

The car hasn't had a service for two years. You can expect it to be a problem to start in the mornings.

Though, in this example, the author similarly connects the two statements, the second statement is one that they are trying to persuade us to believe is true. It is not a given fact, but a prediction (that might not be correct).

Explanations can, of course, be used in an attempt to persuade us of something.

The car hasn't had a service for two years. It often doesn't start in the morning. Regular servicing of cars is important to ensure reliable performance.

The author has moved beyond the fact that this car 'often doesn't start in the morning' to a general point about the need to have cars serviced regularly. The explanation is used in order to produce an argument.

We will meet explanations in another form when we are evaluating arguments. In that context, an author will take a piece of evidence and seek to give an explanation for it. For example, someone might take the evidence that the US has the highest rate of people in prison in the world (which is true) and provide an explanation for it – that the US police are the most efficient in the world at catching criminals (which might not be true).

5

WHAT FORMS CAN ARGUMENTS TAKE?

SIMPLE FORMS OF ARGUMENT

The simplest form of an argument is one with only two parts.

> *Malawi has the highest rate of people injured or killed on the roads of all the countries in the world. So people who go there need to take great care when driving.*

The first sentence is the **reason** for what the author says in the second sentence. This second sentence is what we call the **conclusion** of the argument. This is not because it is the end of the argument, but because it is where the author wanted, so to speak, to end up. This argument still makes the same sense if you reverse the order of the sentences.

> *People who go to Malawi need to take great care when driving. It has the highest rate of people injured or killed on the roads of all the countries in the world.*

You will notice that the word 'so' has been omitted from the first sentence, even though this sentence is still the conclusion. It is obvious why: it would read very strangely to have a 'so' at the beginning of a sentence before anything has yet been established. (In a sense, we go back and put it in once we have read the argument.)

Malawi's very high serious road accident rate is used to make the statement that people who go there should take care when driving. You can see that the flow of the argument is in that direction because it would not make sense in the other. Whichever way round the sentences are put, the order of thinking is the same. Just try the order of thinking the other way round.

> *People who go to Malawi need to take great care when driving. So it has the highest rate of people injured or killed on the roads of all the countries in the world.*

We can represent a simple argument with one reason and one conclusion like this:

$$R \rightarrow C$$

This shows the order of thinking, that the reason *leads* to the conclusion.

ACTIVITY 2

In the following arguments, which is the reason and which is the conclusion?

(1) The percentage of 15 year-old girls in the UK who drink alcohol each week is the highest in the world. There needs to be a campaign to educate girls about the dangers of drinking.

(2) For the sake of their health, people should give up smoking. The campaign to get people to use nicotine substitutes should be increased.

(3) In a few years' time, very few people will use a camera that is not digital. Digital cameras are increasingly popular.

(4) Some of the trees in the park have been cut down. We need to plant some more to replace them.

SIMPLE FORMS OF ARGUMENT WITH MORE THAN ONE REASON

Many arguments that you will come across have more than one reason. They can still have a simple structure, even though there are two or more reasons. The following argument illustrates this:

> *The UK produces more oil than it consumes. The US, on the other hand, consumes more oil than it produces. In the event of an oil shortage, therefore, the UK should be in a better position than the US to deal with it.*

In this example, the first two sentences provide reasons for the conclusion in the third. Because both of the reasons are needed for the conclusion we would represent the structure as:

$$R + R$$
$$\downarrow$$
$$C$$

This structure shows that each of the reasons is needed for the conclusion to be drawn. The reasons act jointly. To show how they do this, consider what happens when one of them is absent.

The UK produces more oil than it consumes. In the event of an oil shortage, therefore, the UK should be in a better position than the US to deal with it.

You can see that the conclusion simply cannot be drawn without the extra information about the US that the second reason had provided. (The same effect is clear when the information about the UK is absent.)

The next example also uses two reasons.

Modern cars are increasingly being fitted with a wide range of safety features. They also often have many luxury features such as very good sound systems. Motoring today is a better experience than it was years ago.

The conclusion in the third sentence is, as in the previous example, supported by the two reasons in the other sentences. However, though the conclusion is drawn from the two reasons, it could have been drawn from either of them. In this way, we can see that the two reasons act independently. We can represent this structure as:

in order to show the way in which the reasons act without each other.

Just to show how these reasons act independently, look at the conclusion in relation to any one of the reasons.

Today's cars often have many luxury features such as very good sound systems. Motoring today is a better experience than it was years ago.

As you can see, the conclusion can still be drawn with just one of the reasons.

There is, of course, no limit to the number of reasons that an argument can have.

Modern cars are increasingly being fitted with a wide range of safety features. They also often have many luxury features such as very good sound systems. Over the past few years, cars have been built to be very responsive to the driver. Motoring today is a better experience than it was years ago.

In the example above, there are three reasons. Again, they act independently of each other, such that the conclusion could be drawn from any one of them. Its structure, of course, would be:

Arguments with more than two reasons can have a combination of those that act jointly and those that act independently.

ACTIVITY 3

Read the following arguments (all of which happen to have something to do with health). In each case, firstly work out which part of the argument is the conclusion. Then decide whether the reasons that are given work jointly or independently.

(1) It is inadvisable for people with a family history of mental illness to smoke cannabis. The risk of suffering from mental illness is doubled for those who smoke cannabis. People with a family history of mental illness have a higher risk than normal of being mentally ill themselves. c

(2) Men who take vitamin supplements are found to have lower rates of cancer. This effect was not found in women. A programme of getting people to take vitamin supplements should target only men.

(3) People who go into work when they are ill (even when they have something as minor as a cold) can double the risk of having heart disease. In addition, going into work when you are ill risks spreading infections (such as colds or flu) to other staff. People who are ill are better to stay at home rather than go to work.

(4) The more people there are who live alone, the greater the problem of a housing shortage. The increasing trend for people to be living alone is one that is worrying. Furthermore, there is evidence that people who live alone suffer worse physical and mental health than those who live with others.

THE NATURE OF CONCLUSIONS

As we have seen, the conclusion of an argument is what, in the end, the arguer wants to persuade us to accept. In that an argument is meant to be persuasive, its author will present at least one reason to support the position that they want us to accept.

FINDING CONCLUSIONS

Again, as we have seen (especially in Activity 3), the position of the conclusion in an argument will vary from argument to argument. It can be anywhere from the first to the last sentence; it can be only part of a sentence; it can be spread over more than one sentence.

Sometimes the conclusion will be flagged up by a word like 'therefore', 'thus', or 'so'. Other words could be 'in consequence', or 'as a result'. The wording of the conclusion itself might well include some words that will give a clue that a conclusion is being drawn: for example, 'should', 'must', 'need to', and 'ought' (and their negatives). However, sometimes the conclusion has to be worked out from the argument without any such clues.

> *Getting people to work less and spend more time with their family (what's called getting the 'work-life balance' better) is often being put forward as a good idea. But it isn't necessarily. In a recent survey, 78 per cent of working people in Britain said that they would not want to reduce their working hours if this meant they would get less money. Indeed, almost a third of the 78 per cent said that they enjoyed their job too much to want to cut their hours.*

In this example, the conclusion is the second sentence. There are no clues at all from the words (only four of them). What you can also see is that the full meaning of the conclusion has to be worked out using the first sentence as well (in order to make it clear what 'it' refers to). You could write this conclusion as:

> *It isn't necessarily a good idea to get people to work less and spend more time with their family.*

You will see that this is what, in the end, the author wants us to accept.

Looking for conclusions where there are no obvious clues in the words used can be made easier if you put a word like 'so' or 'therefore' in front of different parts of an argument (normally each sentence). In the previous example, we come across the conclusion before there are any reasons to support it. Try it with 'so' at the beginning of each sentence.

> *Getting people to work less and spend more time with their family (what's called getting the 'work-life balance' better) isn't necessarily a good idea. In a recent survey, 78 per cent of working people in Britain said that they would not want to reduce their working hours if this meant they would get less money. Indeed, almost a third of the 78 per cent said that they enjoyed their job too much to want to cut*

their hours. So getting people to work less and spend more time with their family is often being put forward as a good idea.

Looking at the argument like this should make it clearer which is the conclusion. What had been in the original passage the first sentence (now put in as the last) doesn't fit like a conclusion at all. This is because there's nothing in the rest of the passage that would lead you to conclude this.

Getting people to work less and spend more time with their family (what's called getting the 'work-life balance' better) is often being put forward as a good idea. But, in a recent survey, 78 per cent of working people in Britain said that they would not want to reduce their working hours if this meant they would get less money. Indeed, almost a third of the 78 per cent said that they enjoyed their job too much to want to cut their hours. So getting people to work less and spend more time with their family isn't necessarily a good idea.

What had been the second sentence fits very well as a conclusion because, unlike with the first sentence, what follows it supports this statement.

Getting people to work less and spend more time with their family (what's called getting the 'work-life balance' better) is often being put forward as a good idea. But it isn't necessarily. So, in a recent survey, 78 per cent of working people in Britain said that they would not want to reduce their working hours if this meant they would get less money. Indeed, almost a third of the 78 per cent said that they enjoyed their job too much to want to cut their hours.

Concluding that 78 per cent of working people said this does not fit with the rest of the passage. In fact, normally we would not expect to find evidence as the conclusion. It is most often given as either a reason or something that supports a reason. This same comment would therefore apply to looking at the final sentence as a possible conclusion. *'So almost a third of the 78 per cent said that they enjoyed their job too much to want to cut their hours'* does not fit as a conclusion drawn from the rest of the passage.

DRAWING CONCLUSIONS

We talk about **drawing a conclusion**. This tells us a lot. The word 'draw' is not used in the sense of making an image, but in the sense of 'taking out from' (as in 'drawing money out of a bank account' or 'drawing water from a well'). A conclusion is the taking out from the reason(s) the point the author wants to make.

> *If you win the jackpot in the National Lottery, you'll be rich. Being rich is what most people hope to be. So people should play the National Lottery each week.*

The conclusion of this argument is taken from the two claims that are made. The author sees them as having this significance.

Continuing this sense of 'drawing' a conclusion, there is a way in which a conclusion could be 'overdrawn'. If your bank account is overdrawn, then you've taken more out of it than you've got in it. In the same way, an overdrawn argument takes more from the reason(s) than is in there. The argument about the National Lottery above gave us a conclusion that could be drawn from the reasons given, without being 'overdrawn'. But what about the next argument?

> *Happy people tend to be richer than those who are unhappy. So being rich makes you happy.*

In the example above, the author has taken the evidence about happy people to mean more than it might allow. Their conclusion takes the evidence to mean a causal relationship – being rich makes you happy – but the evidence need not mean this. As a result, the conclusion cannot safely be drawn from the reason that's given. It is in this sense 'overdrawn'. To emphasise this point, consider the way in which the same evidence could produce a totally different conclusion.

> *Happy people tend to be richer than those who are unhappy. So being happy makes you rich.*

Though it might be argued that the first version of the conclusion looked more likely than the second, the point is that technically the evidence provided could be seen in both ways. This problem highlights the way in which each conclusion could be 'overdrawn'.

DRAWING INTERMEDIATE CONCLUSIONS

Just as arguments can have more than one reason, they can also have more than one conclusion. In an argument with, say, two conclusions, the author will have drawn one conclusion on the way to drawing the final one. We call such 'on the way' conclusions **intermediate**. They are drawn on the way to drawing the 'main' conclusion. Though there can be only one main conclusion, there is no limit to the number of intermediate conclusions. Look at the next example:

European countries are facing many problems as a result of their very low birthrates. The level of immigration helps to some extent to increase the population, but it isn't enough. Thus European countries can't expect immigration to solve all their problems of under-population. So European governments need to encourage people to have more children.

Here we have an argument with both an intermediate and a main conclusion. We can break the argument at the intermediate conclusion to see what is going on.

R: European countries are facing many problems as a result of their very low birthrates.
R: The level of immigration helps to some extent to increase the population, but it isn't enough.
C: Thus European countries can't expect immigration to solve all their problems of under-population.

As you can see, we have a completed argument. The conclusion is drawn from two reasons (acting jointly). This is a significant point about looking for intermediate conclusions: they complete an argument (even though the wider argument continues). To find one, you need to be sure that what you take to be an intermediate conclusion could be taken as the end of an argument (as we have done above).

But, of course, the argument continues in the original to provide a further conclusion. This means that our conclusion – 'thus we can't expect immigration to solve our problems of under-population' – becomes a conclusion drawn on the way to developing the argument further.

R: European countries are facing many problems as a result of their very low birthrates.
R: The level of immigration helps to some extent to increase the population, but it isn't enough.
IC: Thus European countries can't expect immigration to solve all their problems of under-population.
C: So European governments need to encourage people to have more children.

If you look at the structure of this argument, something significant about this argument will appear.

R + R
↓
IC
↓
C

What you can see is that the main conclusion is drawn, not directly from the reasons, but from the intermediate conclusion. In that, as we have seen, conclusions are drawn from reasons, the significance of this is that the main conclusion is drawn from the intermediate conclusion acting as a reason. In other words, the argument could be reduced to:

> *European countries can't expect immigration to solve all their problems of under-population. So European governments need to encourage people to have more children.*

You could, in turn, extend the argument such that the main conclusion became an intermediate one.

> *European countries are facing many problems as a result of their very low birthrates. The level of immigration helps to some extent to increase the population, but it isn't enough. Thus European countries can't expect immigration to solve all their problems of under-population. So European governments need to encourage people to have more children. Therefore, they should give very generous financial incentives (such as tax credits) to couples in order to encourage them to have at least two children.*

In this version of the argument, we have two reasons, two intermediate conclusions, and a main conclusion. The structure looks like this:

R + R
↓
IC
↓
IC
↓
C

Again, you can see that we reduce the last part of the argument to be a reason for a conclusion.

> *European governments need to encourage people to have more children. Therefore, they should give very generous financial incentives (such as tax credits) to couples in order to encourage them to have at least two children.*

What we have seen so far about intermediate conclusions is two things.

- They complete an argument (within an argument).

- They act as a reason for a further conclusion (another intermediate one or a main one).

Something further can happen with intermediate conclusions. Look at a new version of this now familiar argument.

> *European countries are facing many problems as a result of their very low birthrates. The level of immigration helps to some extent to increase the population, but it isn't enough. Thus European countries can't expect immigration to solve all their problems of under-population. So European governments need to encourage people to have more children. An effective way of encouraging people to do things is to pay them. Therefore, such governments should give very generous financial incentives (such as tax credits) to couples in order to encourage them to have at least two children.*

In this version of the argument, an additional reason has been put in. This combines with the second intermediate conclusion to enable the conclusion to be drawn (perhaps with greater force). The structure now becomes:

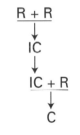

Given so many reasons and intermediate conclusions, it is often helpful to give numbers to the different parts of the argument. This would work as follows.

> *R1: European countries are facing many problems as a result of their very low birthrates.*
> *R2: The level of immigration helps to some extent to increase the population, but it isn't enough.*
> *IC1: Thus European countries can't expect immigration to solve all their problems of under-population.*
> *IC2: So European governments need to encourage people to have more children.*
> *R3: An effective way of encouraging people to do things is to pay them.*
> *C: Therefore, such governments should give very generous financial incentives*

(such as tax credits) to couples in order to encourage them to have at least two children.

If you are writing out the structure using this numbering, it would look like this.

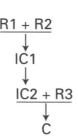

ACTIVITY 1: COMMENTARY

1 There is no argument going on here. There is disagreement obviously, but no part of this conversation gives us a reason to believe that 'everyone is so selfish these days'. 'It's what I think' does no more than make it clear that the speaker is giving their opinion. Furthermore, the first speaker doesn't do anything with their first statement: they don't go on to argue anything on the basis of it.

2 Again we have a disagreement here, but no argument. This disagreement as to whether *Coronation Street* or *Eastenders* is the best soap on TV is not resolved, and we are given no reasons to believe either is the best. Again, as with (1), the author doesn't go on to do anything with the statement about *Coronation Street* (such as 'so people should watch it').

3 Interestingly, with this one, there is no disagreement. But, perhaps surprisingly, there is an argument. The first speaker uses the point that dogs need walking every day as a reason to believe that dogs are less suitable as pets for old people. They have in this way given us an argument that dogs are less suitable pets. The fact that the second speaker agrees makes no difference to whether or not an argument has been presented.

4 This dialogue provides neither disagreement nor argument. The second speaker doesn't dispute that Volvos are both safe and reliable, and the first speaker doesn't provide anything that would enable us to argue that Volvos have these qualities. Once

again, nothing is done with the statement about the safety and reliability of Volvos (such as 'so people should buy them').

5 This dialogue also provides no disagreement, but this time there is an argument. The first speaker does something with the information about vegetarians. They say that people should be vegetarian because of this information about health and longer life. The second speaker's comment does not add to the argument, even though the first speaker uses it to produce their argument.

6 In this example, there is both disagreement and an argument. But the argument doesn't come from the disagreement. The argument consists in what the first speaker says: they give a reason (we can't afford to pay pensions) why people should be allowed to work beyond the normal retirement age. The second speaker's disagreement is irrelevant to the argument. Of course, they could have produced their own: 'people working after the normal retirement age will take up jobs needed for younger people'. Notice the difference between this example and that in (5). In this example, the author puts their argument in the opposite order to that in (5).

ACTIVITY 2: COMMENTARY

1 The first sentence is the reason for the conclusion in the second. The need for a campaign to educate girls about the dangers of drinking is based on the evidence of the high rate of girls who drink. It would not work the other way round, with the need for the campaign leading us to conclude the evidence in the first sentence.

2 Though both sentences make a recommendation, the first sentence gives us the reason for the conclusion in the second. Because people should give up smoking, they should be encouraged to use nicotine substitutes. The order would not fit the other way round.

3 The second sentence provides a reason for the prediction contained in the second. The present increasing popularity of digital cameras leads to the conclusion that few people will use any other camera in a few years' time. If you reverse the order, you have something that might look as if it could be an argument, but it works less well. Predicting the future in order to draw a conclusion about the present would be an unusual way of arguing. However, you could see it in these terms:

In a few years' time, very few people will use a camera that is not digital. So (that must mean that the evidence would indicate that) digital cameras are increasingly popular.

The words added in brackets focus on how the evidence on the present use of digital cameras would have to be seen. As you can see, though you might want to interpret the argument in this way, it works better as an order of thinking if it is reversed.

4   The first sentence is the reason for the conclusion in the second. The need to plant some trees comes from the fact that some have been cut down. The argument would not fit happily the other way round, with our need to plant some trees as replacements serving as a reason for the fact that we've cut down trees down.

ACTIVITY 3: COMMENTARY

1   The conclusion is the first sentence. It is drawn from the evidence presented in the other two sentences. Both pieces of evidence have to be used to draw the conclusion. In this way, the reasons act jointly to support the conclusion.

2   The conclusion is the third sentence. Since the conclusion makes the recommendation about vitamin supplements for men only, we need both reasons to argue in this way. Thus the reasons act jointly.

3   The conclusion is the third sentence. Since it could be drawn from either of the two reasons, they act independently. They give separate reasons why people who are ill should not go into work.

4   The conclusion is the second sentence. The conclusion that the increase in the numbers of people living alone is worrying is drawn from the first sentence (there will be a housing shortage) and from the third (there will be an increase in sick people). In that these reasons provide separate support for the conclusion, it could be drawn from either of them.

2

CREDIBILITY OF EVIDENCE

WHY IS CREDIBILITY AN ISSUE IN CRITICAL THINKING?

Having seen that Critical Thinking is centrally concerned with arguments, what is it about arguments that requires us to look at credibility? The term **credibility** refers to believability. For example, to what extent is the evidence presented in an argument believable? Or, just as often, how believable is the evidence that could be used in an argument? To put it simply, how likely is the evidence that is available to be true?

It can be seen then that an argument that uses evidence (of whatever sort) has to be judged (at least in part) by the believability of that evidence. Thus, any possible strength in an argument could be reduced if the evidence is not believable. We do other things with evidence later, such as looking at the significance of percentages, but with credibility we are faced with the question: how believable is the evidence that is available? This question can be unpacked:

- How believable is the source of the evidence?

- How strong is this evidence?

- How do we decide between opposing evidence?

In this section, we'll be looking at how we would answer all of these questions.

To illustrate the issue of credibility, we'll look at a small example.

95% of the readers of the magazine 'Our Royal Family' said that the monarchy is a 'very good' institution. So all those people who say that the monarchy is no longer relevant must be wrong.

As you can see, this is in the form of an argument. Our assessment of it is essentially one which looks at the credibility and the significance of the evidence.

How credible is the evidence about the readers of 'Our Royal Family'? Given that the readership is almost certainly one that supports the Royal Family, it is highly believable. So does this make it a strong argument? The answer is 'no'. The problem with the argument is that, because the evidence concerns a group of people who are very likely to be unusual in their opinions on the Royal Family, the relevance of the evidence is of limited value. Quite simply, the readers of the magazine are very likely to be biased.

We have seen, then, that the reason that credibility is an issue in Critical Thinking is that it is concerned with the assessment of evidence, evidence that could be (or is) used in arguments.

CREDIBILITY OF REPORTS

Each day **reports** of events are presented to us via newspapers, TV and radio, the internet, from friends and family, and so on. How are we to judge these reports? The answer depends on the nature of the reports themselves. If you pick up today's newspaper, is it believable? If you hear the news on the radio, is it more believable? If you check Ceefax or Teletext, are these also believable?

An example of a report of an event is the football match in August 2005 between England and Denmark. There are different levels at which we can approach credibility of the reports on the match. Which of the following would we say are entirely credible?

- The score was Denmark 4 England 1.
- Wayne Rooney scored England's goal.
- The defeat was partly the fault of the England goalkeeper, the 'flop David James' (*The Daily Mirror*).
- England did not play particularly well in the first half (according to *The Times*).
- 'It was probably one of the worst games I've had for my country.' (Wayne Rooney, according to *The Sun*)

The score in a football match is almost certainly going to be credible. It is a simple piece of information, and any reports on the match have no reason to get that wrong. So, in some types of reports, factual information is going to be entirely credible. But, as we shall see, in other types of reports, it is less likely to be so credible.

Who scored England's only goal is, again, a piece of information which should be entirely credible. There is no reason to suppose that the report is unreliable. Again, as we shall see, such questions as 'who did what?' are not always so easily answered. Crucially, both the score and the fact of who scored the goal are pieces of information that it is difficult to see why they should be given incorrectly. There is nothing to be gained from anyone distorting these facts.

We have moved away from straightforward fact to a judgement when we look at who was to blame for the defeat. In that all the main UK newspapers saw the goalkeeper David James as at least part of the problem, the report by *The Daily Mirror* is not the only one that makes this judgement. In cases like this, remember that, though it's a judgement that's being made, it's one that could be assessed by looking at certain types of information about what happened during the game. It will not surprise us to hear that, shortly after the match, the website of Manchester City, David James' club, stressed his many strengths as a goalkeeper.

The Times was again making a judgement in their report on the game. It is one that was supported by other reports, so was uncontroversial. It is, of course, based on some sort of definition of what we mean by 'playing well' that other reports would presumably agree on.

The comment from Wayne Rooney is significant only if it has been reported correctly. Whether or not it was probably one of the worst games he had ever played for England is a matter of judgement. But whether or not he said it is not. He either did or he didn't. The fact that *The Daily Telegraph* reported him as saying it was 'just about the worst game I've had for England' raises the same point. Did he say both of these things? Did he say one but not the other? Did he say neither of them? This problem highlights something that we will meet later. Even if first-hand sources (as in the case with Wayne Rooney himself being quoted) are used, this does not guarantee that they are being quoted accurately.

Before we leave this football match, consider whether the report of someone who was a spectator in the ground in Copenhagen that night is more credible than someone who watched it on the television at home. Both are in an important way witnesses. But is one more reliable than the other? The obvious answer is likely to be that the person at the ground is more reliable. But, as you might know, being at a football match (or any similar event) can be a problem in always being able to keep up with the detail of what is happening.

Watching a match on television is also a problem in that you see only those parts of the game that you are given, but at least you can see them all without obstruction. So eye-witnesses come in different forms. A report of this match written by an eye-witness is not necessarily a completely accurate guide as to what happened.

HOW CONTEXT CAN AFFECT CREDIBILITY

The problems that we might have in assessing reports such as those of a recent football match are, of course, very small compared to assessing reports of things that happened some time ago, things that happened over a much wider area than a football pitch, and things that happened in a place that most of us can never see directly (such as on a different planet).

Reports of events in the less recent past

We'll consider first of all reports of events that are much less recent. The football match reports were written very shortly after the game had finished. The people from the newspapers who wrote them probably wrote them within a couple of hours of the final whistle. If we wanted to judge reports that took place some years ago, we would have more problems. How would this game compare, for example, to a match in which Denmark beat France 17-1? This might be difficult to judge. The game was played in 1908.

Very abruptly leaving football behind, we're going to consider a report written in 1946-1947 about events happening in 1940-1943. This is a report written by Rudolf Höss. He was the first commandant of the notorious Nazi concentration and extermination camp, Auschwitz. When he was captured after the war, he wrote his autobiography whilst he was in prison. This document is important for a number of reasons. From our point of view, it is important in that it provides an account of what went on in this place. So many witnesses of what happened there are, of course, unable to give us their reports, so we are always going to have an incomplete picture.

How reliable would be the report by Höss on what happened at Auschwitz? Would it be more or less reliable than that given by someone who survived the camp, or by one of the few who escaped? Would it more reliable than reports of what went on in the camp written by the greatest historian of the Holocaust, Martin Gilbert (who wasn't there)?

We'll consider one small part of Höss's autobiography.

'For a while we kept the Gypsies who were capable of work in the base camp at Auschwitz. They did their utmost to get a glimpse of their clan-mates from time to time, even if only from a distance. We often had to carry out a search after roll-call for homesick Gypsies who had cunningly slipped back to join their clan.'

An important part of the context that we need in order to make a judgement of this report is information about Auschwitz. People often think that it was a single camp in one place. In fact, there were a number of camps, the biggest one being what was called Birkenau where most of the large-scale killing (especially of the Jews) went on. What Höss is describing is Gypsies in Auschwitz apparently trying to get a glimpse of, and slipping back to, their families in Birkenau. What is significant is that the two camps are three kilometres apart and that the penalties for escaping from Auschwitz (even if one could) were so severe that the notion of 'slipping' to another camp three kilometres away is a difficult one to accept.

So here we have someone with obviously detailed knowledge of the situation describing something that seems very unlikely to be true. In some cases where this happens, it could simply be that they have forgotten details. This seems almost impossible to believe in this case, in that the context of distance and penalties for escape make it pretty well impossible for Höss to have forgotten them. Perhaps there's a different reason. Shortly before the above account of Gypsies, Höss wrote about a 'large playground' in which Gypsy children 'could run about to their heart's content and play with toys of every description'. Though it is known that such a playground was created (a month before the camp was liquidated), it is very unlikely that sick and starving children ever made much, if any, use of it. Thus Höss might well be describing something that makes things look much better than they were. Remember that he wrote his account after he had been captured and probably wanted to make his crimes seem less than they were. (Other examples include him talking about awful things happening when he wasn't there, even though he probably was.)

In this case, then, the context of when it was written is likely to be very relevant to evaluating the significance of the account (Höss awaiting trial for war crimes). In addition, we have the context that we can check the likely truth of what has been written. We *know* that Birkenau is three kilometres away from the main Auschwitz camp, because it's still there and we can see that it is. Also, Höss himself writes of the dreadful punishments that awaited those who tried to escape.

In this context then we have an eye-witness report, but written by someone who has good reasons to make things look better than they were. These good reasons, therefore, provide something of the context itself. However we interpret things, Höss was hanged at Auschwitz in 1947.

Reports of events taking place on a large scale

Reports of events that took or take place on a large scale present other problems. If, for example, you have a report of the state of Afghanistan, you have the problem of knowing how accurate this report can be. It is a country with 652,000 square kilometres (the UK has 243,000). The majority of Afghans don't have access to clean water or electricity, and for some villages in the mountains the nearest road is two weeks' walk away. As a result, the context of an undeveloped country which has a large geographical area creates problems for credibility of reports of what's going on in the country. If we add in the problem of the fact that certain parts of the country are very unsafe, then the difficulty of credibility is made worse.

But, even when the scale isn't as big (in every sense) as that of Afghanistan, then there could still be problems. On July 1st 1916, at 7.30 in the morning, the Battle of the Somme began with British troops pouring out of their trenches and advancing towards the German lines. The British soldiers thought that the German lines had been destroyed by artillery fire, but they hadn't. By the end of that July day, some 60,000 British troops are reported to have been killed or wounded. How can we be sure of this? The problem of time comes up again as part of the context. How can we check this figure? What sort of information would we need? The context gives us accounts of people who were there, but in the chaos of the battle, perhaps they under-estimated or over-estimated the numbers. Something like this, happening on a large scale, presents problems for credibility.

Even if we can solve the problem of the numbers in this case, there's still the problem of being able to be sure that any eye-witness accounts of what went on during that battle could be said to be typical. When Sergeant Yates of the West Yorkshire Regiment is quoted as saying 'The experience of my platoon was an average one', might there be problems in understanding what was average for that battle?

The solution could be to collect as many eye-witness reports as possible in the hope that, together, they presented a credible account. So, as a rule of thumb, the more eye-witnesses you have, covering as wide a range of situations as possible, the more credible the account is likely to be. But what happens when there are no eye-witness reports?

Reports of events where there are no eye-witnesses

An obvious example is that of what happened to the Mars Beagle 2? There is a long history of failed missions to Mars. Though the Americans and Russians had been sending spacecraft to the planet since the 1960s, if Beagle 2 had landed successfully, it would have been only the fourth example. As it was, everything went well until it landed on December 25th 2003. Unfortunately, no signal was received from it. The British team that had built Beagle 2 were confident that this was a temporary problem and that soon it would start communicating. However, it never did. Various explanations were considered. There could be problems with the Martian weather; the on-board clock was faulty. The first was, in the end, shown not to be case; the second was rejected when attempts to restart the clock by sending an instruction to the craft's computer had no effect. It was then considered that Beagle 2 could well have fallen down a crater, whose high sides stopped the signal being sent. In the end, the scientists in charge of the project decided that it was a dust storm that had caused the problem. Such storms, it was argued, heat up the atmosphere, making it thinner. This thinner atmosphere affected the instruments on board Beagle 2, such that crucially, as it descended at speed, the air bags and parachutes might have opened too late or not at all, meaning that the craft crashed on to rather than landed softly on the surface of Mars.

What we are relying on here are the skills and knowledge of the scientists involved in trying to solve the problem. The context gives us huge problems in establishing the most credible account of what happened. Mars is a minimum of 35 million miles away. We can't just go and check to see what happened. But do we have to accept the explanation of the scientists? Does the context give other things that we could consider? It's very, very expensive sending a spacecraft to Mars. So the scientists wouldn't want their chance of sending another one there affected by being seen to have made mistakes with this one. As in other contexts, then, there are reasons to present the 'truth' in ways that benefit those presenting it.

Reports of events from the non-recent past, on a small-scale, with eye-witnesses

Just to show that, even when events take place on a small scale, with eye-witnesses, it might still be difficult to establish the truth, we'll briefly consider an event that took place in 1922. It is a love story.

Edith Thompson and Freddie Bywaters fell passionately in love. Unfortunately, Edith was married to Percy Thompson. In that the young Freddie worked on a cruise ship, he was away from England for much of the time. In consequence, much of their romance was conducted secretly by letter. Though she asked him not to, Freddie kept Edith's letters (presumably to read time and time again as he sailed the Indian Ocean thinking of her). When he came back to England in the autumn of 1922, they met and renewed their (largely) secret affair. One night, Edith and Percy went to the theatre in London, caught the train back to Ilford, and then walked back from the station towards their house. Freddie appeared and, in a fight with Percy, killed him with a knife. The next day, Freddie was arrested. Shortly after that, so was Edith.

Freddie was charged with murder, and Edith with conspiracy to murder. (Her letters had talked about what looked like attempts to kill Percy with things such as poison in his tea and a broken light bulb put into his porridge.) After the trial, they were both found guilty, and sentenced to death. They were hanged in separate prisons, at exactly the same time on a January morning in 1923.

Edith maintained her innocence right to the end. A huge public campaign to stop her execution had no effect. Reports indicate that she had to be drugged, and then dragged to the gallows. Freddie always insisted that Edith did not know that he was going to confront Percy on their way back from the station.

So here we have eye-witnesses, a very small-scale event, and some fairly obvious ways of looking at credibility. We even have the detailed transcripts of the trial. It should be straightforward.

Edith *would* say that she was innocent (to save herself). Freddie *would* say that she was innocent to save her (because he loved her). Freddie *would* say that he didn't intend to kill Percy, just to confront him (because he didn't want to be convicted of murder).

So it looks all rather an open and shut case. But it isn't as simple as that. The letters that Edith wrote to Freddie (that crucially seemed to show her plan to kill Percy) could be interpreted in lots of ways. There was never any evidence that Percy had at any time been actually poisoned. Freddie's claim that he confronted Percy from the front (and in the ensuing struggle stabbed him) was crucially rejected by the prosecution who argued that Percy's wounds proved he had been attacked from behind. However, in the inquest evidence (which you can still read in the Public Record Office in London), you can see that the evidence did fit with Freddie's account. The first wounds were to the front, showing that he had not jumped on Percy from behind. Is there any reason why such evidence would be distorted? Is there any reason why the prosecution at the trial would not use it?

So what really happened? Obviously we'll never now know. But the case shows that just because people have got very good reasons to lie (given the context), it doesn't mean that they do.

The man who was Edith's executioner killed himself a few years after the execution, claiming that he was convinced that he had 'hanged an innocent woman'. The context of this case now includes another eye-witness. It starts getting very complicated.

So context is important. It highlights all sorts of issues concerned with credibility. We'll be looking at these issues in more detail.

ISSUES OF PERCEPTION, LANGUAGE, INTERPRETATION, AND JUDGEMENT

These issues focus our attention on all sorts of problems in establishing credibility. To ask 'is this report credible?' requires us to look at them.

- **Perception** is concerned with how information, events, and other individuals or groups involved in a particular scenario are seen. This includes literally seeing, but also hearing and experiencing. How much of what was going on in Auschwitz did Höss see? How much of the Battle of the Somme did individual soldiers see or hear or experience? Does the inability of the Beagle 2 team to perceive anything in these senses make it impossible for them to decide what happened? The fact that Freddie Bywaters struggled with Percy Thompson meant that he had perceived the event in every sense. Does this make his evidence very strong as a result?

- The issue of **language** in looking at credibility is concerned with how information and events are described. A good example is how what is called a 'terrorist' attack will often involve the use of words like 'cowardly', 'crazed', 'innocent', and 'victims'. As a result, the event itself takes on a significance that reflects such words. The credibility of reports is then affected by the way in which information is, so to speak, filtered through the language. Can we take seriously the statements of 'insurgents' and 'terrorists'? How do we approach Nazi accounts of 'special treatment' when they mean 'extermination'?

- **Interpretation** of the significance and meaning of facts and events is important in establishing credibility. What does this fact that I have seen mean? If I see someone climbing a ladder in order to get into a house by a bedroom window, what am I seeing? If I know the owner of the house is away, what does this do to my interpretation? Going back to Beagle 2, what is the significance of the fact that, a few days after the disappearance of the landing craft, the US landed two craft on Mars which have both functioned perfectly? Is there any significance at all? The forced evacuation of Israeli citizens from what's called the Gaza Strip in August 2005 was interpreted by Iran's Supreme Leader, Ayatollah Ali Khamenei as being nothing to do with negotiations, but 'as a result of resistance from the Palestinians'. President Mubarak of Egypt saw it as reflecting well on the Israeli Prime Minister, Ariel Sharon, who he described as 'brave and daring'. Can it be both of these things?

- Through perception and interpretation, we arrive at **judgement**. We have perceived events, have interpreted them to mean something, and then we make a judgement of what happened. To what extent is this judgement limited by perception and interpretation? To a large extent, obviously.

CREDIBILITY OF EVIDENCE

We have looked at issues that arise in assessing the credibility of reports. We focus now on the **credibility of evidence**. Such evidence will normally form part of a report, such that it will be used to support a wider picture.

When judging evidence, we use what are called **criteria** of credibility. We have already met them on our way through looking at the credibility of reports, but we're soon going to look at them on their own. We talk then of criteria of credibility, but if we talk about any one of them, then we're talking about a 'criterion' of credibility, criterion being the singular of criteria.

We'll first of all look at different types of evidence.

EYE-WITNESS ACCOUNTS

We've already considered different examples of eye-witness accounts. Rudolf Höss was an eye-witness; so was Freddie Bywaters. In both cases, we would at one level value their evidence, but also see it as having limitations.

Following accidents or incidents, there are often appeals for witnesses. 'Were you at... on...? If so, please contact...' The belief is that such witnesses might have seen something that is relevant to establishing what happened. The credibility of the report, therefore, is likely to be strengthened by having eye-witness accounts.

As a rule of thumb, of course, this is true. If you saw the accident, then your evidence is almost certainly going to be more relevant than mine if I didn't. But eye-witness evidence still has potential limitations.

- An important limitation is that we have to take it that eye-witnesses saw (heard, experienced) things accurately. There could be all sorts of reasons why they didn't (distractions, obstructions, etc.).

- Another important limitation is that we have to take it on trust that eye-witnesses reported what they saw and heard, etc. accurately.

- Going on from this, we have to take it that they are reporting things as they saw and heard them. In other words, they reported things honestly (rather than distorted them for a reason).

- A further limitation is that, even if eye-witnesses see and hear, etc. things accurately and then report accurately, they still might be reporting on something that was not typical of the whole event. Thus, if the event is on a large-scale, their evidence might be very limited (although relevant to that small part of the action).

REPORTING

Most of us read eye-witness accounts as reported by someone else. An obvious example is the reading of a newspaper report in which eye-witness reports are quoted or referred to. They might even be as anonymous as 'an eye-witness said'. Reporting raises similar issues to eye-witness evidence. It could be that the report is one of inaccurately-perceived, inaccurately-described, and unusual events. In this way, reporting can add to the problems of credibility by adding another level of possible distortion. The person putting the report together could select eye-witness accounts that fitted with what they wanted to say. In doing so, they might deliberately leave out those accounts that don't in this sense fit. For all you know, I could have missed out crucial eye-witness accounts of what happened when Freddy Bywaters killed Percy Thompson.

Reporting is, of course, more than just collecting eye-witness reports. It involves the collection of information relevant to the subject of the report. Judging the credibility of a report involves looking at the issues of:

- selection (including omission) of information;
- the editing of this selection;
- the interpretation of the selected information;
- making a judgement based on this interpretation.

You should be able to see that credibility problems arise in many ways in judging the significance of a report.

REPORTING OF REPORTING

This takes the problems through another stage. A report of a report (or a report of a number of reports) very much raises the issues of selection (including omission), editing, interpretation, and judgement. With regard to selection and omission, someone putting together a report based on other reports could decide to select only those reports (or those parts of them) that fitted with the direction they wanted their report to take. They could also, of course, use information based on a report without intending a deliberate distortion, believing that the original report was accurate.

A good example of this was what happened following the reporting of a debate which took place in April 2005 on the subject of using animals in experiments. One of the speakers was a man called Mike Robins who spoke in favour of animal experiments. He suffers from Parkinson's disease, a disease of the central nervous system which affects movement and control over limbs. He argued that he could control the tremors he suffered as a result of a 'deep brain stimulator' which had been inserted. The person who inserted the stimulator, Professor Tipu Aziz, claimed that research on monkey brains had led to the development of the stimulator (a claim which was disputed by another expert at the debate, Professor Claude Reiss).

On May 15th 2005, *The Observer*, a UK Sunday newspaper, ran an article on this part of the debate with the headline 'Hundreds shouted at me, roll over and die'. The content of the article included the following:

> *'I was bayed at,' said Robins, a retired naval engineer from Southampton. 'Several people were shouting. Some called "Nazi!", "bastard!", and "Why don't you roll over and die!" I tried to speak, but was shouted down. It was utterly terrifying.'*

The writer of the piece was Robin McKie, the Science Editor of *The Observer*. McKie was not at the debate, so was using an eye-witness account as the basis of his report on what happened.

However, there were other eye-witnesses, and more than that, there was a video recording of the proceedings. The other eye-witnesses disputed Mr Robins' version, as did the video-recording. Here was the first point of significance. The May 15th article used evidence from only one eye-witness. The whole business of interpretation and judgement was based on this.

The other evidence resulted in *The Observer* running a further article entitled 'Two sides to animal rights story'. In this article they make a number of useful points that are useful for a credibility analysis.

- *'Crucially, the paper was not present at the debate but interviewed Mr Robins afterwards.'*

- *'Straightaway, we can see that the headline was inaccurate. In his own words, hundreds did not shout 'roll over and die'. I contacted Mr Robins who told me that while there may not have been hundreds in the room (there were 150) his perception was that hundreds were shouting at him.'*

- *'The difficulty here is the difference between his perception – held, and reported, in good faith – and the reality, as displayed in a video recording of the meeting, made by Europeans for Medical Progress (EMP), organisers of the debate.'*

- *'Various other eye-witnesses were quoted, saying that what was reported did not happen: 'I heard nothing untoward.' 'I cannot understand why you want to distort the truth to such a ridiculous degree.' 'To state that people in the audience shouted at Mike Robins "roll over and die" is fiction.'*

Summing things up, this second article stated

'Even allowing for this disparity in the versions of events, our story was unbalanced, in that it failed to include any comment from the anti-vivisection side of the debate.'

This second article therefore addressed what turned out to be important credibility issues about the first article. This first one is a very useful illustration of the potential problems of using one eye-witness account, or even of seeing such accounts as necessarily more significant than other types of evidence.

But the story does not stop there. In that we are considering the issue of reporting of reports, what is significant here is that the original article (now shown to be 'unbalanced') is still being used as an accurate account. For example, if you search the internet for 'Mike Robins Animal Rights', you'll find many examples of where the original article has been reported in other reports as if it were accurate.

We can summarise in a diagram what we've been looking at so far. We start with the event, whatever it is. As we move from left to right, we see changes in what the event is seen as. Each move, represented by a change in the font, represents the way in which perception of the original event can change. The final **Event** is therefore different from the original Event.

Event → **Eyewitness** → *Report* → REPORT OF REPORT = ***Event***

OTHER SOURCES OF DATA

The previous example included one piece of evidence that was different from the others we have been considering. This was the video-recording of the debate. This can be seen as an eye-witness account without the obvious problems we have so far identified. It has no axe to grind, no point to make. But it isn't entirely without problems. There is, so to speak, at least one person behind the video-recording. Someone is doing the recording, possibly selecting different parts of the hall where the debate was taking place at different times. Furthermore, the tape that's produced could have been edited. In this sense, though a video-recording is a very important source of data, it is not without some scope for distortion.

By 'data' we are here meaning, pieces of information. A video-recording shows (assuming no distortion) what was happening at various times during an event. CCTVs (close circuit televisions) provide information on what's going on in areas where it is seen as necessary that there is some surveillance of what people are doing. Thus we find them in shops (to discourage and identify shoplifters), in prisons (to check on what prisoners are doing), in some parts of our towns and cities (to discourage crime, and to identify people who commit it), and so on. CCTV evidence provides data, information that is expected to be reliable. Pity, then, the foolish young criminal who broke into a Manchester shop that sold CCTV equipment and was photographed very clearly by eight security cameras.

In the same category, of course, there are photographs themselves. Video- (including CCTV) recordings are no more than a series of photographs. Photographs could be used as important sources of information. They supposedly capture what was happening at a particular point in time.

However, photographs are less reliable than they might seem. The famous case of Kate Winslet's legs getting reduced by airbrushing for a magazine cover is a recent example. But there are much older ones. In the Soviet Union, there were many cases of political figures who fell out of favour with the leader Stalin. Photographs which showed them appearing with the leadership were changed, when they fell out of favour, such that it looked as if they'd never been there.

In this way, photographic evidence is useful, but not conclusive. All sorts of things can affect the value of such evidence.

- There are technical issues concerned with the effects of different cameras and lenses, such as the way panoramic cameras can distort the angles of buildings.

- There is the way in which a photograph could be 'set up' to look as if something was happening when it wasn't. (Years ago, if you wanted a divorce you had to prove adultery, that you'd been unfaithful with someone, so photographs were taken of you with someone prepared to pose as if the two of you had been caught in the act.) One of the most famous examples of the 'set-up' problem was the case of the Cottingley Fairies. In 1917 two cousins claimed to have taken photographs of fairies in their garden. There were five photographs in all, four of them showing fairies appearing with the girls. A local expert in photography was shown the photographs and declared that they were genuine, unretouched images. The pictures caused a national debate with various prominent people being convinced that they were indeed genuine. In fact, it was not until 1978 that some sort of evidence that they weren't genuine emerged. Someone noticed that the fairies were almost identical to those that had appeared in a children's book of 1915. In 1981 the two cousins admitted that four of the photographs were fakes, but insisted that the fifth (the one that showed just fairies without the girls) was a genuine image. So here we have photographic evidence that was seen as sufficiently credible for serious articles to be published in the 1920s, arguing that they proved that fairies existed. A modern parallel is, of course, apparent photographic evidence of UFOs. Do such photographs lend strong support to the argument for the existence of UFOs?

- There is the possibility of the image being just part of the original. Perhaps things have been missed out in the final image, thus changing the significance of what appears.

- With modern photographic techniques, single images can be created that are a composite of all sorts of separate images. Does this mean that photographic evidence is becoming less and less credible?

Another source of data is what are called flight data recorders and cockpit voice recorders (known as 'black boxes' in aircraft, even though they're painted orange). The first of these records information such as airspeed, fuel flow, altitude; the second records conversations between the pilots, and between the pilots and air traffic control. Thus if an aircraft crashes, these black boxes will provide evidence of what was happening just before the crash. Sources of data such as this provide very reliable information. Of course, people have to listen to the stream of information that comes out of these recorders and interpret it, but problems of bias are probably few in that the interpreters probably have no reason to distort their interpretation. Plans to include video-recorders as part of the cockpit recorders will make this evidence even more useful.

CREDIBILITY AND BIAS

We have already considered ways in which the credibility of reports, and evidence in them, can be unreliable. In short, there can be a problem of **bias**. The word 'bias' means 'prejudice' or 'influence' or 'distortion'. If you are biased, then you are more likely to go one way rather than the other. Thus, if you are unbiased, you are not prejudiced, influenced to go one way or the other, and your evidence, interpretation, and judgement are not distorted. As you can see, bias is at the very heart of credibility issues.

Bias can appear in many forms.

ACCIDENTAL BIAS

There could be all sorts of reasons why evidence and reports based on it could be accidentally biased.

- People might think that evidence is reliable when it isn't. For example, they might not be aware of problems with the evidence, such as the sample was too small, the timescale of the research might have been too short, and so on.

- The evidence might come from a normally reliable source. The example in the next section on 'Deliberate bias' regarding Sir Cyril Burt illustrates this well.

- It might be widely-reported. The earlier example of *The Observer* and Mike Robins shows reports using the misleading, but widely-reported first version.

- They might have accidentally ignored other evidence, not being aware of it. Perhaps the other evidence has been published somewhere you wouldn't expect to find it.

DELIBERATE BIAS

Accidental bias will, of course, produce distortion and will still therefore make any report biased in this way a problem for credibility. Deliberate bias produces distortion that is intended. The author of the report or the evidence wants us to believe something, though they know it not to be true.

The types of deliberate bias are many.

- Evidence might be presented that is not true. The prosecution case at the Thompson and Bywaters trial seems to have deliberately misled the court over the nature of the injuries to Percy Thompson.

- Evidence might be selected and omitted such that one case is supported, even though the complete evidence does not support it.

- Evidence might be invented. Our Cottingley fairy girls are an example. There have been other bigger events in history. The burning down of the Reichstag (the German Parliament building) in 1933 was blamed by the Nazis on the Communists in Germany. Almost certainly, the evidence linking them to it was fabricated; Hitler's own people very probably started the fire. A very interesting controversy that is still going on concerns the claim by the psychologist Sir Cyril Burt that intelligence is inherited rather than determined by our environment. When he died in 1971, Burt was seen as one of the most important educational psychologists of his time. However, the following year questions were being asked as to whether his results could be trusted. He was accused of making up some of the data he used to support his argument. In 1979, his biographer concluded that Burt had knowingly used fraudulent evidence. (More recent work has questioned this.)

- Evidence that is collected can be interpreted in ways that fit with what is intended. The official inquiry into who killed President Kennedy in 1963 was accused of doing this, interpreting the evidence to fit with the official verdict that only one man, Lee Harvey Oswald, was involved in the assassination.

As you can see, whether the bias is accidental or deliberate, an argument that is based on such evidence will be overdrawn.

JUDGING CREDIBILITY: POSSIBLE WEAKNESSES

VESTED INTEREST

This term is one that you will often find yourself using in looking at the credibility of evidence and reports. It is used to describe a weakness in the credibility. This is because of the meaning of the term. If I have a **vested interest** in something happening, then I stand to gain in some way if it does. This could affect the way in which I provide evidence or put together a report.

Vested interest always has two components:

- what the vested interest is in;

- why we would say that there is a vested interest.

Going back to Sir Cyril Burt, we might say that, because he had a vested interest in proving that intelligence was inherited (given that he had built his reputation, in part, on claiming this), he had a vested interest in falsifying his results to show this.

There is another more recent example.

Over the past few years, there has been a considerable controversy over the MMR vaccine. MMR refers to measles, mumps, and rubella. A vaccine combining protection for children against these three very serious diseases is normally given to children. However, in 1998, an article appeared in *The Lancet*, one of the most influential and prestigious medical journals in this country (and throughout the world), which questioned the safety of this vaccine. Specifically the authors of the article, including Dr Andrew Wakefield, argued that the MMR vaccine increased the risk of children developing autism and an inflammatory bowel condition. This led to many parents refusing to allow their children to be vaccinated.

Allegations were subsequently made against Dr Wakefield that suggested that his research findings were questionable. It was found that he had received funds from lawyers who were acting to help support claims that the MMR vaccine was linked with autism. This information was not made available to his co-authors or to the editors of *The Lancet*. The editor of the journal concluded that there was 'a fatal conflict of interest' and that, if it had been known beforehand that funding was an issue, the journal would not have published the article.

In this example, vested interest is taken to have reduced the credibility of the evidence.

However, just because there is evidence that there could be vested interest, this does not mean that there will be. Someone might well have the possibility of benefiting from a course of action, but still not adjust their evidence such that the result favours them.

This means that when you are faced with assessing some material using credibility criteria, and you think that vested interest might be present, you will need to explain how this is so. You could do it in two ways:

- X has a vested interest to lie about what happened because she can't risk losing her job.

- X has a vested interest to lie about what happened because, if she did send out the wrong material, she risks losing her job.

In the first version, we have explained why X has got a vested interest (this is important). In the second, we have explained why X has got a vested interest using a hypothetical reason. We look at hypothetical reasoning in detail in Section 6, but we can note that using it in credibility exercises can be very helpful. What we are doing is giving *possible* reasons why there might be a vested interest. Such hypothetical reasons could be in different forms:

- X has a vested interest to lie about what happened because, supposing she did send out the wrong material, she risks losing her job if this was found out.

- X has a vested interest to lie about what happened because, unless she sent out the right material, she risks losing her job if it was found out that she didn't.

What we are doing in each case is to explain the circumstances in which X would have vested interest. We could even contrast one vested interest with another.

- X has a vested interest to lie about what happened because, if she did send out the wrong material, she risks losing her job. However, she also has a vested interest to tell the truth, if she did send out the wrong material, in that she knows that the company can be sympathetic to people making mistakes if they own up to it, but not sympathetic if they lie about it.

In summary, then, we can list the things that you should always consider when using vested interest as a credibility criterion.

- Just because someone could have a vested interest, this does not mean that this will affect their behaviour.

- We need to know how vested interest could affect behaviour (what will it make someone do: lie, tell the truth, steal the money, cheat, and so on?).

- We need to know why someone has got a vested interest. What is it in the particular context that is relevant? (Lose a job, be seen as reliable, can't pay their bills, be seen as successful, and so on.)

- We need to know under what circumstances the vested interest will 'kick in'. (If they have done/not done something, and so on.)

JUDGING CREDIBILITY: POSSIBLE STRENGTHS

When we are judging credibility, we need to be aware of the way in which evidence and reports can sometimes be seen as strong because they are highly believable. We will look at three ways by which evidence and reports will be strengthened if any of them is present.

NEUTRALITY

The criterion of **neutrality** applies when at least one of the sources of evidence or reports has no obvious reason to take one side or the other. The fact that they might take one side or the other will be due to other factors. It is, then, the opposite of vested interest.

The word 'neutral' is often applied to countries. When we talk of a neutral State, we are talking of a country that doesn't take one side or the other in war. In World War Two, both Sweden and Switzerland were neutral. They didn't fight on either side, so didn't actively get involved in the conflict. So was Ireland. The word is also applied to cars. 'Neutral' gear means that the engine is disconnected from those parts of the car that make it move. The engine isn't going to take the car forwards or backwards when it is in neutral gear.

Thus someone who is neutral isn't going to favour one side or the other. If they do, when they have no reason to do so, then they have ceased to be neutral.

In what sort of situations would we expect to find such neutral people or evidence? An obvious example is in a game like football, rugby, or cricket. A referee or umpire's job is to interpret and apply the rules of the sport in a way that is fair. They should not favour one side or the other.

A very famous football match was the one in 1998 between England and Argentina which resulted in the sending off of David Beckham for (softly) kicking one of the Argentinean players. The referee was Kim Milton Neilsen from Denmark. This is an obvious point: to achieve neutrality, you wouldn't expect to have a referee from the same country as one of the two teams. Neilsen has explained how he approached his job.

'Whatever had happened between the teams in the past was not important because a referee has to start from zero and focus on that game.'

This is a very good way of putting it. A neutral person starts 'from zero'. There is no prior vested interest that they bring to the situation, no loading of things in one direction or the other.

What other people start 'from zero'? You would expect to find this in any competitive situation. It's when you don't find it that you would be particularly concerned, because the importance of neutrality is very high. When a French and a Russian judge were alleged to have cheated in the 2002 Winter Olympic figure-skating competition, the whole business of the judging system in such an event could be weakened. The French judge admitted that she had been pressured into voting for the Russians, so she had not voted 'from zero'.

When else would we expect to find neutrality? We would expect to find it when someone or some organisation is brought into a situation in which, again, they have no vested interest to support one side or the other. For example, in disputes between employers and trade unions or employees, an organisation called the Advisory, Conciliation, and Arbitration Service (ACAS) is often brought in to work with the two sides. The only vested interest ACAS has is to get an agreement between the two sides. A recent example of their work was to try to solve the London Underground dispute.

In the same way, we would think of Environmental Health Officers, Health and Safety Officers, and other similar positions as being neutral. They seek to solve problems by just interpreting and applying the rules in a neutral way.

What is the importance of finding a neutral person or organisation in assessing the credibility of evidence or reports? Finding neutrality in this way is important because of the absence of vested interest. The force of this is that we would normally expect to be able to trust their evidence. The only problem could be accidental bias (as considered above), so this means that we should still consider the possibility of distortion. But the lack of any deliberate bias is significant. If our neutral organisation or person says that they think that X is the case, then we should consider very seriously that X is.

As with vested interest, we need to spell out why we think neutrality is present.

• X is neutral because they have no known vested interest in preferring one outcome to the other.

Thus neutrality could come from:

• the role that a person, group, or organisation performs;

• the fact that a person, group, or organisation has no obvious or known vested interest.

EXPERTISE

What might an individual, a group, or an organisation have if we say they have **expertise**? The term covers a number of different things.

• Relevant training

• Relevant experience

• Relevant knowledge

• Relevant skills

The word 'relevant' is crucial. For example, because Kim Milton Nielsen is an international football referee, he has got very relevant expertise in a football match. Quite simply, he wouldn't be in this role if he didn't have relevant training, experience, knowledge, and skills. That doesn't mean to say that his expertise goes beyond this. If you wanted to find out why the Mars Beagle 2 hadn't functioned, we wouldn't ask him.

This point about relevance is important in another way. This is that the context of the situation needs to allow the person to use their expertise. Let's say someone collapses in a department store. They have a suspected heart attack. A first aider on the staff is called, and does what she can (puts the person in the recovery position, say). A nurse happens to be in the store and responds to a message over the public address system asking for help. She can do more than the first aider, having more expertise. She does what she can. An ambulance is called, but will take about ten minutes to get there. Fortunately, a doctor is also in the store. She has got, in this case, even more expertise than the nurse has. She uses this expertise, applying all her skills, knowledge, and experience to try to help the patient. The ambulance arrives. But the person has died.

Let's change the scenario. Someone has a heart attack whilst they are visiting a relative in hospital. They are quickly dealt with by the cardiac team and survives.

The two situations all involved the role of expertise. A number of different people used their skills and knowledge in a situation in which they were relevant. In the first scenario, the first aider used her skills in an environment that she was trained for (a medical emergency in an everyday situation). The nurse and doctor used theirs in an environment that was missing possibly crucial things (equipment, drugs, etc.) for them to use their expertise fully. In the second scenario, the expertise that was available was able to be used with all the necessary equipment.

What these examples show is that we need to judge expertise in a relative way. Expertise is a relevant criterion if the context allows for it to be used effectively. If our football referee is in a game in which the pitch is invaded by a large number of fans who prevent the game from being played, then his expertise is no longer relevant. The police who arrive to sort things out now have their relevant expertise.

So, when we are looking at the credibility criterion of expertise, we need to ask two questions to see if it is relevant.

1 Does the situation require expertise that is beyond what most people are likely to have anyway?

2 Does the situation enable someone to use their expertise?

1 Does the situation require expertise that is beyond what most people are likely to have anyway?

We have to be careful when applying the criterion of expertise. We are using the term to mean something beyond what we would expect most of us to have. Thus, if we are dealing with a scenario in which there is a dispute as to whether or not a letter was posted, then we couldn't say that someone in the office has got particular expertise in ensuring that it was. This is something that we would expect was widespread knowledge in an office environment.

The scenario therefore gives us the context by which we can judge the criterion of expertise. A barrister has much greater expertise in the law than an estate agent. But, when judging the value of the barrister's house, the estate agent will (should) have more expertise. When a barrister and an estate agent disagree over why the barrister's car won't start, then a motor mechanic will have more expertise than either of them. So, in short, use expertise only when it's relevant.

2 Does the situation enable someone to use their expertise?

Even if someone has expertise, this doesn't mean that they can use it fully. There might be reasons that would stop them being able to use it fully. For example, they might not have the necessary information at their disposal to make expert judgements. They might not be able to see what happened. For example, the attempts to find out if Saddam Hussein had weapons of mass destruction were deliberately obstructed by the Iraqi authorities. In consequence, the experts were not always able to use their expertise to evaluate evidence that would enable them to make correct decisions.

As with other credibility criteria, when you want to apply the criterion of expertise, you need to spell things out clearly.

- X has got expertise relevant to this situation because they have skills, knowledge, training, experience (whatever combination you want) that enables them to make a judgement about it that is an informed one.

Of course, we must consider situations in which expertise is used such that a bad decision is made. A very good example of this is the tragedy of mothers being convicted for murdering their children on the basis of evidence given by Professor Roy Meadow. Professor Meadow was seen as an eminent doctor specialising in the health care of children. In 1977 he published an article in *The Lancet* in which he argued that what are called 'cot deaths' were likely to be the result of a parent killing the baby, rather than a condition which would cause the death. He was frequently called to be an 'expert witness' in cases in which parents (normally mothers) were accused of murdering their babies.

In one case, Sally Clark was accused of murdering two of her babies. Professor Meadow argued to the court that the chances of there being two unexplained infant deaths in one family were one in 73 million. This was a crucial part of the evidence that sent Mrs Clark to prison. However, this piece of evidence was utterly flawed. The Royal Statistical Society calculated the odds to be around only one in a hundred. Though their evidence was initially ignored (how could this renowned expert be so wrong?), eventually Mrs Clark's case was reviewed and she was released from prison. Professor Meadow was himself investigated by the General Medical Council which has the power to 'strike off' doctors who are guilty of 'serious medical misconduct'. They did strike him off, arguing that he had abused his position as a doctor by giving false and misleading evidence. He has been accused by other experts of deliberately distorting his evidence by 'cherry picking' what he uses. In other words, they argue that he chose only those pieces of evidence that supported his argument and ignored those that didn't.

The case of Professor Meadow highlights how expertise can distort credibility when it is used in a way that distorts evidence.

ABILITY TO PERCEIVE

We have already looked, at length, at the significance of the ability to **perceive**. We have looked at why it might be both a strength and, in some circumstances, a weakness. It can be even more of a strength when it is added to one or both of the previous two criteria. Thus, if someone has neutrality, expertise, and was able to see what happened then we would expect to have a very credible account. To illustrate how this might work, let's return to the England v Argentina game of 1998. The referee explains how the ability to see was crucial.

> *There were two early penalties, and the people who debate them forget they are only relying on a camera's angle. The referee is much closer to the action and can see things far more clearly than a particular camera angle. If there had been a camera on the opposite side to show the Michael Owen penalty it would have looked a lot different. It is very difficult to use cameras and expect them to always show you the truth.*

What this shows is that a credibility criterion becomes more significant when it is added to another or others.

JUDGING CREDIBILITY: BOTH STRENGTHS AND WEAKNESSES

MOTIVE

We have already looked at vested interest. As we saw, this can give a motive both to tell the truth and to lie. The term **motive** opens things up beyond the narrower 'vested interest'. When we are assessing the credibility of evidence and reports, we should consider that there are all sorts of motives that individuals, groups, and organisations might have for what they say and do. These motives could be either a source of strength or weakness in the evidence or report. Some examples should make this clear.

- A scientist has a motive for reporting the results of tests he is doing correctly because he is concerned that scientists should always be honest.

- A teacher has a motive to teach her students as well as possible so that, by getting grades that are as good as possible, she can achieve her own ambitions.

- A detective has a motive to solve a serious crime such as murder or rape so that he or she can protect the public from further attacks.

Psychologists might see all of these as examples of 'vested interest' in that, in each case, the individual gets personal satisfaction from achieving from what they have set out to achieve. But they go beyond vested interest as we have been using the term.

Thus you should look for wider motives than purely vested interest. The story of Oscar Schindler, made famous in the Steven Spielberg film 'Schindler's List' is a good one to reinforce our thinking here. Starting off with the motive of making money, Schindler moved into having the motive of saving people. Both might be seen by some psychologists as vested interest, but there seems to be more than this going on here.

REPUTATION

This criterion of credibility is one that very much fits with the idea that some of the criteria can be seen as both strengths and weaknesses. At one important level, **reputation** can be seen as a neutral criterion, which needs context in order to be used.

So what do we mean by the term? Someone's reputation is how they are thought of in terms of their character and/or behaviour. People might see someone as having the reputation for being honest, hard-working, arrogant, unhelpful, and so on. When applied to credibility, we are looking for things like truthfulness, honesty, reliability (and, of course, their opposites). Professor Roy Meadow was seen as a valuable expert witness because he had the reputation of being someone who had carefully researched the subject of 'cot deaths', and had experience of being able to interpret evidence. Obviously his reputation is now very different.

Very often you'll be faced with applying the criterion of reputation to organisations rather than individuals. For example, when we were looking at the Professor Meadow case, we referred to the Royal Statistical Society. If you've never heard of this, you might infer from the name, that this has a reputation for considerable expertise in statistics. The Society was founded in 1834 and has indeed considerable expertise in using and interpreting statistics. Its reputation for long-standing excellence played a big part in the acquittal of Sally Clark and other wrongly-convicted women.

In our earlier example of *The Observer* and the misleading account of what happened at the Oxford debate, we noted that, though the newspaper published a second article admitting their errors, many websites still use the first article as the basis for points they want to make. In part this is because of the reputation of *The Observer* for being a serious, reliable newspaper. Its reputation means that we normally believe what it says.

If we wanted to look into the subject of genetically-modified (GM) crops, how would we assess the 288,000 entries that Google gives us for that subject? Would the reputation of Friends of the Earth for opposing them mean that we wouldn't look at their website for information on GM crops? Would the reputation of the magazine *New Scientist* for covering both sides of the debate make us very likely to check what they've got to say? Would we be particularly interested in the website of the Nuffield Council of Bioethics? This tells us:

> *The Nuffield Council on Bioethics examines ethical issues raised by new developments in biology and medicine. Established by the Nuffield foundation in 1991, the Council is an independent body, funded jointly by the Foundation, the Medical research Council and the Wellcome Trust.*
>
> *The Council has achieved an international reputation for addressing public concerns, and providing independent advice to assist policy makers and stimulate debate in bioethics.*

Good heavens. What a lot of credibility criteria are packed into this. Neutrality ('independent body', 'independent advice'), reputation (an 'international' one), and expertise (which we pick up from context) are all there. So reputation for expertise and neutrality make their contribution to the GM debate (and other debates) very significant.

If we looked at the BBC site, we'll find lots of relevant information about GM. But what reputation does the BBC have? You might have heard of the Hutton Inquiry in 2004. This looked into the death of David Kelly, the Government's weapons expert, who had killed himself following revelations that he had, without permission, talked to the BBC about weapons in Iraq. The BBC reporter Andrew Gilligan made allegations about what the Government had supposedly done with some evidence relating to such weapons. The Hutton Enquiry concluded that the BBC had not acted with sufficient care over the story, and the BBC's reputation for reliable reporting was diminished. So do we still see the reputation of the BBC as sufficiently high for us to see their reporting as always credible?

Reputation is therefore a criterion that can go both ways. Evidence and reports need to be assessed, where relevant, by looking at the reputation of those who supply them.

It can apply in very small situations as well as the large ones we have been considering. If we had a scenario in which there is a dispute as to what happened in a classroom when the teacher was out of the room, it could come in there. The student who had a reputation for being a bully might be less believable than someone who had a reputation for telling the truth, when they are both asked why one of the students has got a bloody nose.

Again, we need to be explicit about how we are applying the criterion.

• X has got a reputation for doing/being P, so their evidence is likely to be believable/unbelievable.

JUDGING A CASE

In the end, after looking at our credibility criteria, we are faced with making a decision. So is this scenario more likely than another one? Is this person to be believed more than another one? Is it more likely that this happened or that something else happened?

Looking back at some of the examples we've considered:

• Did Freddie Bywaters mean to kill Percy Thompson, or did he mean only to argue with him?

• Did the Beagle 2 not function because of a dust storm or because of poor design?

• Did two girls photograph fairies in the 1920s? Or was even the fifth photograph a fake?

We'll look at other criteria that we need to use to start putting a case together.

CORROBORATION

This is a term that invites us to look to see if one statement is supported by another. The word has its origins in a Latin word that refers to 'strength'. If your account of what happened is the same as mine, then our accounts are made stronger. It's like an alibi in court. If I say that I wasn't at the scene of the crime at the time in question, and there is evidence (like CCTV footage) that I was somewhere else at this time, then my defence is strengthened.

So, when we are looking for **corroboration**, we are looking for statements that support evidence or claims. We're not looking for evidence that just sees that one claim is on the same side as another. We're looking specifically for more than one piece of evidence or one claim that is saying the same thing. My defence that I wasn't at the scene of the crime at the time the crime was committed is not helped by someone saying that I'm a kind and thoughtful man. They might be on my side, but my statement isn't corroborated by theirs.

If you think back to the Freddy Bywaters evidence, his claim that he confronted Percy Thompson from the front is corroborated by the forensic evidence that the first wound was to the front of Thomson's neck, not the back.

The claim by the two girls in the Cottingley fairies case that their photographs were genuine was corroborated by the local photographic expert who could find no evidence of their being 'retouched'.

As we have just done, when you are asked to provide examples of corroboration in preparing your judgement, you should be very clear about exactly what is being corroborated.

- X's claim that P happened is supported by Y's claim that P happened.

- X's claim that P didn't happen is supported by Y's claim that P didn't happen.

Corroboration is often found between people on the same side, but it need not always be so.

- X's claim that P happened is supported by Y, even though they disagree on whether Q happened.

CONFLICT

Conflict is simple to understand. It is the opposite of corroboration. Thus, just as with corroboration, we were looking for points of agreement, now we're looking for points of disagreement.

Again we can illustrate from our previous examples.

- Mike Robins' claim that 'hundreds of people shouted at me, "roll over and die"' is in conflict with the evidence that only 150 people were in the room. It is also in conflict with the video-recording of the proceedings, and various eye-witnesses. (Of course, the latter two corroborate each other.)

- The claim by Rudolf Höss that Gypsies at Auschwitz could see those in Birkenau and could 'slip' back to the latter is in conflict with the evidence that Birkenau is three kilometres away from the main Auschwitz camp (and the penalties for escaping).

- The claim by Edith Thompson that she hadn't planned to kill her husband is in conflict with the content of some of her letters that give details of what appear to be at least two examples of when she did.

The force of conflicting evidence is that it weakens the significance of evidence. If Sir Cyril Burt did falsify some of his results in order to show that intelligence is inherited, this would suggest either that he had some evidence that conflicted with this, or that the absence of supporting evidence could be seen as conflicting with this.

As with corroboration, we are looking for sufficiently detailed examples when you refer to conflict.

- X's evidence that P happened is in conflict with Y's evidence that P didn't happen.

- X's evidence that P didn't happen is in conflict with Y's evidence that it did.

Just as corroboration allowed for disagreement between people on the same side, so too does conflict allow for agreement on some things with people on different sides.

- Though X and Y disagree on whether or not P happened, they do agree that Q happened.

IDENTIFYING SIDES

In the end, once you've looked at material in order to judge credibility, you'll have an idea as to who's on what side. Is it more or less likely that X happened is a question that will divide your sources of evidence. Thus in our Mike Robins example, we would have the following division.

More likely that 'hundreds shouted "roll over and die"'

- Mike Robins

- Robin McKie (in first article)

Less likely that 'hundreds shouted "roll over and die"'

- Video-recording of the debate
- Eye-witness 1
- Eye-witness 2
- Eye-witness 3

That's all we're doing by identifying sides: creating two lists. If there are any neutral characters who don't support one side or the other, then we could either have a third list 'Neither more nor less likely…' or we put the two lists next to each other, showing our neutral sources/people in the middle. So, when you're asked to give the balance of evidence, you need to do no more than identify the sides.

LOOKING FOR THE WEIGHT OF EDVIDENCE

The Critical Thinking assessment uses the bag of apples approach to establishing the **weight of evidence**. In other words, the more apples you put in a bag, the heavier it is. Applying this to our lists that identify sides, we are simply adding up the numbers. So, just by doing that, with four sources of evidence supporting the 'less likely' case and only two supporting the 'more likely' case, we judge that the weight of evidence is greater for the 'less likely' case. It's no more than that, than counting apples in two bags (or three, if we have any neutral apples).

DOING THE CREDIBILITY CALCULUS:
EVALUATING THE QUALITY OF EACH SIDE

Having counted the number of apples, we're now going to look at the apples more closely. The heavier bag might have more rotten ones; it might have smaller ones; it might have fewer tasty ones. So now we're going to make some judgements of quality.

The method we're going to use is not one that'll be asked for in the exam. We're doing it here to help us to see how a picture of credibility is built up by making judgements about the evidence that's presented.

We're going to take each of the criteria we've been looking at and try to give them a numerical value. This isn't what we were doing in looking at the weight of evidence, in which each source or person was given the same value regardless of any credibility criteria.

We'll start with the **ability to perceive**. We spent some time considering how this could vary from source to source. There could be those eye-witnesses who could perceive everything that was going on; there will be those who can perceive everything in front of them, but what they perceive is only part of the wider scenario; there will be those who will perceive only some of what is in front of them (as a result of distractions, obstructions, etc.)

We can give the ability to perceive a score of 1–3, such that we have the following:

0: source was not an eye-witness

1: source could perceive only some of what happened

2: source could perceive everything that happened, but what happened was only a part of the wider scenario

3: source could perceive everything that happened (and this was the complete scenario)

When we use **expertise**, we could use the following scheme:

0: no relevant expertise

1: limited expertise (little experience, knowledge, etc.)

2: some expertise (some experience, knowledge, etc.)

3: considerable expertise (much experience, knowledge, etc.)

When we use **vested interest**, we need to take into account that this can both strengthen and weaken credibility. If it weakens it, then it will be a minus figure; if it strengthens it, it will be a positive figure.

0: no vested interest

1: a little vested interest

2: some vested interest

3: considerable vested interest

For example, if the vested interest reduces credibility than the score of 2 could represent 'some vested interest to lie, be selective with evidence, etc.' It would then become –2.

When we use **reputation**, we could use the following:

0: no relevant reputation

1: little reputation of…

2: some reputation of…

3: considerable reputation of…

Again, as with vested interest, reputation can be a weakness in credibility as well as a strength. Someone who has a considerable reputation for not telling the truth would give us a score of –3; someone who has a considerable reputation for honesty would give us a score of +3.

With **neutrality**, we would have the following:

–1: not neutral

+1: neutral

This indicates the difficulty of there being degrees of neutrality. Perhaps it's simpler just to classify sources as being neutral or not.

In applying this framework, we will arrive at an overall figure for credibility. Each set of material could have a maximum figure based on the number of sources and the number of relevant credibility criteria. However, in that we're dealing with the credibility of the accounts that we're given, it's simpler to use just raw figures.

To make the process of calculating more straightforward, we'll give each criterion a signifying letter:

A: ability to perceive

B: expertise

C: vested interest

D: reputation

E: neutrality

If we revisit the Mike Robins material, the credibility calculus would work like this:

Mike Robins: A = 2 (being at the front, he might not have heard everything correctly); B = 0 (no relevant expertise); C = –2 (some vested interest against the group that opposes animal experimentation; we could even have this as –3); D = 0 (no relevant reputation); E = –1(not neutral)

Robin McKie: A = 0 (wasn't there); B = 3 (science editor of *The Observer*, so should have lots of expertise in writing the report); C = –2 (some vested interest in the account being correct); D = 2 (reputation for fair reporting, could be 3)

Overall total = +2

Video-recording: A = 2 (presumably not everything shown); B, C, D = 0; E = +1

Eye-witnesses: if we treat each one the same, we get A = 2; B = 0; with vested interest, we could have a mixture C = –1; 0; +1; D = 0; with neutrality, we could have a mixture, E = –1; +1; –1. The score for these eye-witnesses would be the individual scores multiplied by 3. This gives us +5.

Overall total = +6

The credibility calculus shows that it is much less rather than more likely that 'hundreds shouted "roll over and die"'.

This method offers all sorts of ways of enabling us to make judgements about the credibility of evidence and reports.

For the exam, you will need to turn this credibility calculus back into words. Thus you will write about how one side has perhaps more expertise than the other; how vested interest is more obvious on one side than the other; how one side crucially has a neutral source. In this way, you will be writing about the quality of the evidence on each side.

MAKING A JUDGEMENT

Then, at last, you come to a **judgement**. Like we did using the credibility calculus, your judgement will be what is more likely to be the case. You can't say for sure what the truth is, but you can say (and will need to say) what, on the basis of doing all that we have done, is the most likely. Guilty or not guilty. You decide.

Sources

Höss: *KL Auschwitz seen by the SS*, The Auschwitz-Birkenau State Museum, 2005, p.52

Somme: *Somme*, Lyn Macdonald, Papermac, 1983, p.243

England v Argentina 1998 match (Kim Milton Nielsen): BBC News website

3

ASSUMPTIONS

ASSUMPTIONS EXPLAINED

So far we have looked at arguments in terms of their reasons and conclusions. More specifically, we have looked at reasons that the author has actually stated, what are sometimes called *explicit* reasons. But arguments normally contain more than what is actually or explicitly stated. They also contain **unstated reasons**. (Just as stated reasons are called explicit reasons, so unstated reasons can be called *implicit* reasons.) This is perhaps a rather odd idea. But the next example should make it clear what we mean by an unstated reason.

Gorillas are highly endangered. Therefore we should try to save them.

As you can see, this is a straightforward argument. The conclusion doesn't look in any way overdrawn. But the argument works only because other parts of it are playing an important role. These are beliefs that the author must have, even though they haven't stated them. The author appears to conclude that we should save gorillas only on the basis that they are endangered. But this conclusion also requires that the author believes, for example, that:

The loss of gorillas is something that we don't want.

You can see how this statement fits with the reason to enable the author to draw the conclusion. You might say that the statement is obvious, but you can also see that the author doesn't state it explicitly.

We call these missing parts of the argument **assumptions**. They are what the author has, if you like, taken for granted. They haven't felt the need to state them. There is nothing unusual in an argument having assumptions as part of it. There is also nothing suspicious about an author not making all their reasons explicit. We all do it, for the very simple reason that we don't feel the need to state everything explicitly. The argument about saving gorillas is a good example of this. When you first read it, you probably didn't see it as an argument with a problem. This was because, in a way, you read it as if the author *had* said 'The loss of gorillas is something that we don't want'.

It is worth repeating the point that assumptions are those parts of the argument that the author *hasn't* actually written or said. There is a way in which the word is used differently in everyday speech. So, someone might say, 'A-levels used to be really hard years ago. They're much easier these days'. And you might reply 'You're just assuming that. You haven't proved it'. Here the word 'assuming' is used to mean that the arguer hasn't given any evidence for something they've said, has just said something. As you can see, this everyday meaning is the exact opposite of how it is used in Critical Thinking. In our example about gorillas, it would be like saying that the author assumes that 'gorillas are highly endangered'. They might not have proved this, but crucially they have stated it, so can't be said to have assumed it.

Look at the next argument.

> *The trains are severely delayed again. Lots of people are going to be very late for work.*

Again, this simple argument is straightforward. But you might be able to see that the author has to believe something that they haven't stated.

> *There are no practical alternative means of transport for the people who are going to be very late for work.*

Thus, for example, the author must believe that the train company hasn't laid on adequate buses to take people to their destination.

In looking for assumptions, then, we are looking for statements of what the author *must* believe to be true in order to argue as they do, even though they *haven't stated* them. This is a very demanding requirement, in that we have to come up with statements that the author must accept as part of their argument.

FINDING ASSUMPTIONS

If we look again at the previous example, we'll see how an author could dismiss suggested assumptions even if they appear to be relevant to their argument. Look at the following.

> *Not many people use cars to get to work.*
> *The trains are often late.*
> *Most people are not normally late for work.*
> *Lots of people use the trains to get to work.*

Does the author have to accept any of these? Let's look at them one by one.

> *Not many people use cars to get to work.*

Though the author argues that lots of people are going to be late for work because the trains are late, we do not know if the author believes that few people use cars to get to work. Crucially, the reason we don't know this is because their argument doesn't require that they do believe it. For example, they could still argue as they do, even if a large number of people travel to work by car. All the author is concerned with is the lots of people who travel by train. How many travel by bus or car (or even walk) is not something the author has to be specific about.

> *The trains are often late.*

The use of the word 'again' indicates that the trains have been late before this occasion (more exactly, that the author believes it to be true that they have been late before). But the word 'often' is one that the author is not committed to accepting in order to argue as they do. Perhaps the author is talking only about the second time the trains have been late: their argument could certainly be read in this way.

> *Most people are not normally late for work.*

There are two ways in which this statement is not one that the author has to accept. The words 'most' and 'normally' make it a statement that the author could reject without it affecting their argument. All the author has done is to argue about what is going to happen today, based on a problem today. They're not making a prediction based on what normally happens to most people.

Lots of people use the trains to get to work.

The author connects two things in their argument.

(R)   The trains are severely delayed again.
(C)   Lots of people are going to be very late for work.

It is clear that the author is seeing the first as the reason for the second. But to connect them in this way requires that the author sees trains being severely delayed as relevant to 'lots of people'. If very few people use the trains to travel to work, then the argument doesn't work, in that the conclusion doesn't follow. (The most that could be concluded is that 'some people' or more specifically 'a few people' are going to be late for work.) In this way, we can see that the author must accept 'lots of people use the trains to get to work' as true, in order to argue the way they do. We have therefore found an assumption the author must make.

THE NEGATIVE TEST

Being able to apply a test to a statement to see if an argument requires that statement would be a very helpful guide to finding assumptions. Fortunately, there is such a test. We call it the **negative test**. It works very simply. Take a statement that you think might be assumed in an argument, and then turn it into its negative form. If this negative form would prevent the conclusion from being (usefully) drawn, then you have found an assumption.

If we apply it to the examples we've already considered, you should see the power of the negative test very clearly.

Gorillas are highly endangered. Therefore we should try to save them.

We worked out that, for the argument to work, the author had to assume that 'the loss of gorillas is something that we don't want'. What happens when this is turned into its negative form?

The loss of gorillas is something that we want.

This, as you can see, creates a fatal problem for the argument. To be sure that it is fatal, put it into the argument and watch the conclusion collapse.

Gorillas are highly endangered. The loss of gorillas is something that we want. Therefore we should try to save them.

Now try the same test with the late trains argument. But this time put in the negative form of one of those statements we decided were not assumed.

The trains are often late.

If we put this into its negative, we get the following.

Though the trains are not often late, they are severely delayed again. Lots of people are going to be very late for work.

As you can see, we have incorporated the negative without causing a problem for the argument. As a result, we can confirm that the statement 'The trains are often late' is not an assumption the author makes. However, when we put in the negative of the statement that we worked out the author had assumed, we'll see (as with the gorillas example) how the negative test is so useful. This was 'Lots of people use the trains to get to work.'

The trains are severely delayed again. Lots of people don't use the trains to get to work. (Therefore) lots of people are going to be very late for work.

This time, the argument simply doesn't work. Why would lots of people be late for work because the trains are delayed, if they don't travel by train?

Why does the negative test work?

Remember, we are looking for what the author must believe to be true in order to argue as they do. There are two ways in which the negative test can work.

- The first is looking at whether the author is contradictory. It's a problem for anyone's argument to be contradictory. (Just imagine if someone said 'All killing is wrong, whatever the circumstances, so executing murderers is a good thing and should be introduced in this country'.) So believing within one argument, both that something is the case and that it isn't, cannot be accepted. In other words, if we find a statement that creates a contradiction within the author's argument, we've found an assumption (its opposite).

- The second is that if the author could accept both a statement and its negative, without having a problem for their conclusion, then we can't have found something that the author assumes.

For example, look again at the argument about saving the gorillas.

Gorillas are highly endangered. Therefore we should try to save them.

If we came up with the suggestion that the author had to assume

All endangered species should be saved.

using the negative test will give us

Not all endangered species should be saved.

As you can see, the author could accept either of these two statements without there being a problem for their argument.

ACTIVITY 4

In the section on reasons and conclusions, there was an exercise in which you were looking to see which part was the reason and which the conclusion. Look at these arguments again and, for each one, work out an assumption that is needed to connect the reason with the conclusion.

(1) The percentage of 15 year-old girls in the UK who drink alcohol each week is the highest in the world. There needs to be a campaign to educate girls about the dangers of drinking.

(2) For the sake of their health, people should give up smoking. The campaign to get people to use nicotine patches should be increased.

(3) In a few years' time, very few people will use a camera that is not digital. Digital cameras are increasingly popular.

(4) Some of the trees in the park have been cut down. We need to plant some more to replace them.

ASSUMPTIONS AND EVALUATION OF ARGUMENTS

You might sometimes read (or be told) that the more assumptions there are in an argument, the weaker that argument is. This is not correct. An argument could have a lot of assumptions simply because it is a long argument. It could have very few and still be a poor one. Because assumptions are no more than those reasons that the author hasn't stated, they don't in themselves indicate either strength or weakness.

Look at the next example.

> *There is concern about the problem of head injuries in boxing. In some sports, the head is protected from injury, as in American football and ice hockey. Therefore we should require boxers to wear headguards.*

In this example, there is a very simple assumption that the author has made. This is that 'headguards will help to protect boxers from head injuries'. (There is another: 'the use of head protection in other sports is relevant to its use in boxing'.) If you consider the first assumption, it isn't a clear sign of weakness in the argument to believe this. Obviously, there might be evidence that headguards don't protect boxers (although they are used in amateur boxing and in training sessions). But we wouldn't say that the argument was weak because we had found an assumption. Similarly, it wouldn't have made it stronger by making the assumption a stated reason.

This is not to say, however, that finding assumptions can't be used as a way to do some evaluation of an argument. This is because they do tell us more of what an author is arguing. Look at the next example.

> *There is a law that is concerned with what should happen about the problem of dangerous dogs. This law sees a few breeds of dogs, such as pit bull terriers, as being more likely to be aggressive than most others. However, some research on dogs' behaviour questions this belief. The study is of over 300 cocker spaniels and their owners. The evidence shows that owners of highly aggressive cocker spaniels are more likely to be tense, emotionally unstable, shy, and undisciplined than owners of cocker spaniels which are low in aggression. The dogs' aggression must therefore be a response to their owner's personality. Having shown that it is a dog's owner that causes a dog's behaviour, we should not condemn some breeds of dogs as being more aggressive than others.*

Which one of the following does the author of this argument assume?

(A)   There's no such thing as an aggressive dog.

(B)   Laws cannot solve the problem of dangerous dogs.

(C)   Evidence on cocker spaniels and their owners is relevant to other breeds of dogs and their owners.

(D)   People who have cocker spaniels are more undisciplined than people who have other breeds of dogs.

The author doesn't have to assume (A). The argument is trying to explain why some dogs are more aggressive than others, not to dismiss the idea of there being aggressive dogs. The negative test would straightaway show you that the author actually believes the negative version so (A) can't be assumed.

The author criticises the law that's referred to in the argument. This is because it wrongly sees some breeds of dogs (such as pit bulls) as more aggressive than others. However, the author isn't committed to believing that other laws couldn't solve the problem of dangerous dogs (by requiring owners to go on training courses, for example). So the author doesn't have to assume (B). (Try the negative test to check.)

The author's argument uses evidence on cocker spaniels and their owners in order to argue 'Having shown that it is the dog's owner that causes a dog's behaviour, we should not condemn some breeds of dogs as being more aggressive than others.' It can be seen that the author uses *only* the evidence on cocker spaniels and their owners, so must assume that this evidence is relevant to other breeds of dogs and their owners. The negative test would very convincingly show you what happens if the author believes the negative version. Clearly, (C) must be assumed.

The argument makes a distinction between owners of cocker spaniels who are undisciplined and those that aren't. It doesn't therefore see owners of cocker spaniels as being any more undisciplined than owners of other dogs. So (D) does not have to be assumed. As always, try the negative test to check what happens.

This exercise reminds us that, when we find assumptions, we find out more about an argument than we get from just reading it. We are, as you can see, reading more of it in a very real sense. What we did with this argument was to read something that connected the sentence 'The study is of over 300 cocker spaniels and their owners' and the one 'Having shown that it is a dog's owner that causes a dog's behaviour…'

Having found an assumption, what does that tell us about this argument? It shows that there could be a problem with the author's use of this evidence. The problem is that the conclusion is overdrawn. If the author had said something like 'the evidence suggests that a dog's owner might affect the behaviour of a dog, so we should look again at whether some breeds of dogs are more aggressive than others', then the conclusion is much safer. The assumption about cocker spaniels and their owners, of course, remains the same, even with this weaker conclusion. But, finding the assumption took us to the heart of the possible problem in the argument.

Of course, there needn't be a problem in the argument. The author could be entirely justified in their belief that cocker spaniels and their owners are typical of all dogs and owners. Why shouldn't they be? How many different types of breeds and owners would we need evidence on before we accepted either the weaker or the stronger conclusion? Thus, finding the assumption led us to a very important point of evaluation. But, just because the author made this assumption doesn't in itself mean that the argument was weak. Assumptions are useful to find for evaluation, but just being able to find them doesn't tell us whether the argument is weak or strong.

The next exercise, which is on the next page, uses a longer argument and offers seven statements to consider as possible assumptions.

ACTIVITY 5

The various campaigns trying to promote healthy living discourage people from eating chocolate. In fact, people often feel guilty if they do eat it. However, research on the effects of eating dark chocolate has found that it can reduce the effects of a heart attack. This is because it contains very high levels of what are called flavonoids and which improve blood flow. Both blueberries and tea also contain flavonoids, but not at such a high level as dark chocolate. Furthermore, it's often forgotten that chocolate is plant-based (being made from the fruit pod of the cacao tree), just as are the fruit and vegetables that we're encouraged to eat for a healthy diet. Therefore, for the sake of our health, we should eat dark chocolate every day.

What must the author assume in this argument? To make it easier to find out, we need to be clear what is going on in this argument. In its simplest form, the argument structure is as follows.

R1: Research on the effects of eating dark chocolate has found that it can reduce the effects of a heart attack.

R2: Chocolate is plant-based, just as are the fruit and vegetables that we're encouraged to eat for a healthy diet.

C: Therefore, for the sake of our health, we should eat dark chocolate every day.

In order to find an assumption, then, we need to find a statement that links at least one of these reasons to the conclusion.

Take each of the following statements, and consider which of them (there could be more than one) is an assumption the author must make in this argument.

(A) Dark chocolate is sufficiently like fruit and vegetables to be good for our health.

(B) Only products which come from plants are good for our health.

(C) Unless we eat dark chocolate every day, we won't be healthy.

(D) Good health is the only reason to eat dark chocolate every day.

(E) People eat dark chocolate because it's plant-based.

(F) There are no significant health risks with eating dark chocolate every day.

(G) People with healthy hearts eat dark chocolate.

ACTIVITY 4: COMMENTARY

(1) *The percentage of 15 year-old girls in the UK who drink alcohol each week is the highest in the world. There needs to be a campaign to educate girls about the dangers of drinking.*

The author argues from the high percentage of 15 year-old girls in the UK who drink to the need for a campaign to address this problem. To connect the conclusion with the reason, the author has to assume that:

It is wrong/to be regretted/unfortunate/unacceptable that the percentage of 15 year-olds in the UK who drink alcohol is the highest in the world.

In short, if the high percentage isn't a problem, then why is the author arguing that we need a campaign to try to deal with it?

Another assumption you might have come up with is the following:

A campaign to educate girls about the dangers of drinking alcohol will be effective in reducing the percentage of 15 year-old girls in the UK who do.

Putting this into its negative form will quickly show you why this is assumed.

(2) *For the sake of their health, people should give up smoking. The campaign to get people to use nicotine patches should be increased.*

The recommendation that we should increase the campaign to encourage smokers to use nicotine patches is drawn from the reason that 'for the sake of their health, people should give up smoking'. An assumption required by this argument is one that connects smokers giving up smoking with nicotine patches.

Nicotine patches are effective in helping people to give up smoking.

The negative test (Nicotine patches are not effective....) shows that, unless the author believes this to be true, their conclusion sits very oddly as one drawn from the reason.

What about the next one?

Nicotine patches are the most effective way of helping people give up smoking.

In this case, though the author might believe it to be true, we don't know if they do from their argument. In other words, nicotine patches could be the cheapest way of helping people give up smoking. A method such as hypnosis could be more effective, but less easy to provide to lots of people. Thus, our negative test will show us that, though the negative version (Nicotine patches are not the most effective...) sits a little oddly in the argument, it doesn't make the conclusion impossible to draw.

There's one other point to note. The author doesn't assume that 'Smoking is bad for our health' in that they *state* that 'for the sake of their health, people should give up smoking'.

(3) *In a few years' time, very few people will use a camera that is not digital. Digital cameras are increasingly popular.*

The author in this argument is making a prediction based on the present. So some sort of assumption must be made about this. Is it the following?

The present is always a guide to the future.

This is too big for the author, in that they might well think that there are all sorts of examples where the future cannot be predicted from the present. The negative test will emphasise this. So we are looking for a much more specific assumption that allows the particular prediction about digital cameras to be made.

The present popularity of digital cameras is a good guide to their future popularity.

This is something that the author must believe, in that, without this, they cannot draw their conclusion. (Try the negative test.)

Another assumption that you might have come up with is something else that links the present with the future with regard to digital cameras.

Digital cameras will not be replaced by alternative technology.

Though it might be difficult to think of what the alternative technology might be, the author still has to assume this to be true in order to draw their conclusion. (Think of how video cameras and recorders have been replaced.) Try the negative test again to emphasise the significance of this assumption.

(4) *Some of the trees in the park have been cut down. We need to plant some more to replace them.*

The author concludes that we need to plant trees because some have been cut down. This requires an assumption which links the loss of trees to the need for replacements. This leads us to:

The loss of trees in the park is something that is a problem.

Though this looks a little thin as an assumption, you can see that, without it, the author can't connect the reason to the conclusion. The negative test will show very clearly why the author has to assume this.

If you'd come up with a bigger assumption, then the author is not so likely to need to assume it. For example:

Trees shouldn't be cut down.

This is much too big. The author isn't required to accept this at all (there could be, to the author, all sorts of good reasons why the trees had to be cut down).

For every tree that's cut down, another one should be planted.

Again, this is too big for the author. The author isn't even committed to believing that in the case they're describing that the number cut down should be replaced exactly by the number planted (it could be more or less or the same).

Whatever answer you came up with, use the negative test to see whether the author's argument requires it as an assumption.

ACTIVITY 5: COMMENTARY

(A) is assumed. The author uses the fact that chocolate is plant-based to support their conclusion that we should eat it. They emphasise the significance of this fact by linking it to the point that we're encouraged to eat fruit and vegetables for a healthy diet. Indeed, since the force of R2 lies very much in the reference to fruit and vegetables, the author has to assume that the health-giving properties of fruit and vegetables are also found in chocolate. The negative test will show that, if the link between chocolate and fruit and vegetables in R2 is rejected, then the author cannot use it to argue as they do.

(B) is not assumed. The author argues that dark chocolate is good for our health in part because it is plant-based. But this claim does not require that they see only plants as being good for our health. For example, they would have to accept that water is necessary for our health.

(C) is too strong for the author to have to believe this to be true. Though they are recommending that we should eat dark chocolate for the sake of our health, they are not saying that it is a requirement for good health that we do eat it. Quite simply, the author is recommending chocolate as good for our health, rather an essential product for our health.

(D) goes much further than the author has to accept. Though they see good health as the reason for eating dark chocolate, they are not committed to believing that there are not other reasons for doing so. An obvious other reason is enjoyment. Try the negative test here. 'Good health is not the only reason to eat dark chocolate every day' is not a problem for this argument. This statement could be put into the argument without the conclusion being in any way affected.

(E) is not assumed. Though part of the author's argument is that people ought to eat dark chocolate because it's plant-based, why people actually do eat dark chocolate is something that the author is not concerned with.

(F) is assumed. The author concludes that, for the sake of our health, we should eat dark chocolate every day. This recommendation must be based on the belief that, even though it is clear that dark chocolate is good for our health, there are no significant health risks that would make this recommendation a problem. (For example, there are no harmful substances in the chocolate that would work against the flavonoids.) Try the negative test with this one. 'There are significant health risks with eating dark chocolate every day' creates a massive problem for the author's conclusion. Note that, just because we've found this assumption doesn't mean that we've found a necessary weakness. The author might well be entirely right in believing that there are no significant health risks in eating dark chocolate every day.

(G) is not assumed. The author refers to evidence that (and gives an explanation why) dark chocolate reduces the effect of heart attacks. But they are not committed to the belief that eating dark chocolate is a *requirement* for a healthy heart. People could have a healthy heart for all sorts of reasons.

EVIDENCE

ASKING QUESTIONS ABOUT EVIDENCE USED
IN ARGUMENTS

Arguments don't have to use evidence, but they often do. Indeed, an argument can be based entirely on evidence.

> *The number of teenage pregnancies (for girls aged 15 to 17) in 2003 fell by about 10 per cent from the figure in 2001. In 2001 the Government introduced its Teenage Pregnancy Strategy, so the policy of reducing the number of teenage girls who get pregnant must be working.*

In this argument, the author relies on two pieces of evidence (the fall in the number of teenage pregnancies between 2001 and 2003, and the fact that the Government introduced the Teenage Pregnancy Strategy in 2001). Without them there is no argument.

The same evidence can be used as part of a bigger argument.

> *The number of teenage pregnancies (for girls aged 15 to 17) in 2003 fell by about 10 per cent from the figure in 2001. This is good news. Teenagers who get pregnant are likely to do less well in their education and, as a result, reduce their chances of getting good jobs when they are in their twenties. In 2001 the Government introduced its Teenage Pregnancy Strategy, so the policy of reducing the number of teenage girls who get pregnant must be working. The Government should therefore be praised for this.*

In this argument, the author gives us some more evidence: that on education and employment chances for teenage girls who get pregnant. Even though this evidence is much less precise than the evidence on the number of teenage pregnancies and the introduction of the Strategy, it still counts as evidence. The words 'do less well' and 'reduce their chances' indicate that the author is giving us information. What about the sentence 'This is good news'? Here we don't have evidence. We have a judgement. The author has judged that it is good that fewer teenagers are getting pregnant because of the evidence on education and employment. This judgement is then used to draw the main conclusion that 'the Government should be praised' for its Teenage Pregnancy Strategy. (You will see that the previous argument's conclusion has become the intermediate conclusion of this one.)

In the last argument, the author made a judgement of the significance of some evidence. When we say something is good or bad (or whatever), we are going further than the evidence itself. The evidence is, in an important sense, neutral. When we looked at assumptions, we made the same point. You will remember that an assumption is neutral in the sense that it doesn't in itself tell us anything about whether an argument is weak or strong. Evidence is in a way the same. Until an author does something with it in an argument, it is neutral. Look back at the first argument in this section.

The information on the fall in teenage pregnancies is simply that: information. It takes on a significance – that the Government's programme must be working – only when the author develops an argument from it.

So, what we need to do is look at how evidence is interpreted in an argument. In doing this, we are asking the following questions:

• What explanation has the author used for the evidence?

• What significance has the author given the evidence? (What do they think the evidence *means*?)

• Has the evidence got other possible significance (meaning)?

• Is the evidence sufficient for the author to use it in the way they do?

Let's apply some of these questions to the evidence on the teenage pregnancy rate.

• What explanation has the author about the evidence?

The author has taken the evidence to mean, straightforwardly, that the teenage pregnancy rate went down between 2001 and 2003 because of the Teenage Pregnancy Strategy. This Strategy caused the reduction.

- What significance has the author given the evidence? (What do they think the evidence *means*?)

The author takes the evidence to mean that there is no other explanation. They take it to mean that it is strong enough evidence to stand alone in the argument, so that the conclusion can be drawn from it.

- Has the evidence got other possible significance (meaning)?

The evidence could be seen in different ways. (See Chapter 5, Evaluating Arguments for the way in which an author can take one thing to be the cause of another, and the way in which this can be a problem. This appears in the section on what are called *post hoc* arguments on page 94.) For example, the Teenage Pregnancy Strategy might be only one of the possible explanations for the decline in the number of pregnancies. We could think of more. For example, it could be that more girls have decided that education is important to them, so have ensured that effective contraception is used. It could be that there has been a campaign (other than the Strategy) to provide girls (and boys) with information, contraception, and so on.

Interestingly, we don't know if the 10 per cent reduction was a bigger or smaller reduction than expected from the Strategy. A 10 per cent reduction could in this way be consistent with the Strategy not having worked as well as it should. And it is also consistent with its having worked spectacularly well!

- Is the evidence *sufficient* for the author to use it in the way they do?

As we saw with the previous question, we don't know enough about the significance of the evidence to know if the author can use it in the way they do. We would need to know more about such things as whether or not there are other explanations for the 10 per cent reduction (or at least for part of the reduction). We would need to know if, for example, other countries had seen a similar reduction without a Teenage Pregnancy Strategy. If they had, then the reduction could be part of a trend in which girls throughout, say, much of Europe are trying to ensure that they don't get pregnant. Looking at the evidence in a different way, it could be that the 2001 figure for teenage pregnancy was unusually high, so that a 10 per cent reduction did no more than bring the numbers back to a normal level. Of course, if the 2001 figure was unusually low, then the reduction in 2003 is even more impressive.

There is another point to make about sufficiency. Does the evidence provide a complete picture? The figure is given for pregnancies of teenagers between the ages 15 to 17. What about the figures for 14 year-olds? Or even 13 year-olds? Both of these figures are likely to be very small, but they might still show an increase.

There is in this case yet another point to make. Given that we are told that the Strategy was introduced in 2001, we might be surprised if its impact was so dramatic that it took effect really quickly. This emphasises the point that we need to know the figures for the years before the strategy in order to see if the fall from 2001–2003 was no more than the continuation of already declining figures.

In the end, what we're doing when we evaluate evidence is to look at how the author has used it, *what they think it means*. Don't think that we could get away with just saying 'the author might be lying'. This is rarely going to be the case (and never with material in an AS paper). The author might not give the whole truth in the sense that they might give only part of the evidence. As with the example about teenage pregnancy, we have seen that the evidence given does not provide us with the full picture. But, of course, just because the author hasn't given the full picture does not in itself mean that the author is deliberately distorting the evidence.

You might want to say that it is significant that the author doesn't tell us where the evidence comes from. In other words, you might think that, without having this information, we can't judge whether or not the evidence is reliable. Though it might help us sometimes to know the source of evidence, if we don't know it we apply the test of good faith. This means that we take it that the author is presenting the evidence without deliberate distortion, that they are presenting evidence that is as it has either been published or has appeared in some form.

So, when you are asked to evaluate the way an author uses evidence, it is of little or no value to say either that the author might be lying or that you don't know where the evidence comes from. There are, as we have seen, far more important things to say about evidence in an argument.

DIFFERENT TYPES OF STATISTICS

Evidence is presented in different ways, and so it is important to be able to understand the significance of different types.

PERCENTAGES

Evidence is often presented in the form of percentages.

50 per cent of people use honey and lemon in hot water as a way of treating a cold. Only 20 per cent of people use garlic.

This is straightforward. Half of the people in the study used honey and lemon when they've got a cold; only a fifth uses garlic. There's nothing difficult going on here.

Percentages normally have the advantage of us not having to worry about numbers. (That word 'normally' is important as we'll see later.) In the above example, you don't really have to worry about the numbers involved. Even if only fifty people were interviewed, it's still the case that twenty-five of them used honey and lemon for a cold, and only ten used garlic. Of course, percentages give you no idea of the size of the group that's being referred to. In this case, then, you could have had a study of only twenty (or fewer) people. But this shouldn't worry you when it comes to evaluating evidence which is presented as percentages. The significance of the percentage needs to be looked at in terms of how an author has used the evidence in the argument.

We will shortly look at evidence that uses numbers rather than percentages. Be careful that, in your evaluation of percentage evidence, you don't just slip into a comment like, 'we don't know how many the percentage refers to'. Very often, the percentage will tell you far more than the number. This is shown clearly in the next example.

It is increasingly difficult for couples and families to manage without the woman working. For example, couples take out mortgages on the basis that both of them will continue to work. It should not be surprising that 46 per cent of the workforce is female. Therefore, we need to ensure that adequate childcare facilities, such as day nurseries, are available.

If you were asked to evaluate the significance of the 46 per cent, then it would be completely irrelevant to say 'we need to know how many this is'. If you were simply given the evidence '13,156,000 people in the workforce are female', you would probably benefit from knowing what proportion that is of the total workforce (46 per cent). So, in cases like this, the percentage tells us much more than the number can. If you wanted to do an evaluation of the significance of the 46 per cent, then you'd want to know things like what percentage worked part-time in order to assess whether the author's conclusion was overdrawn.

NUMBERS

If you are presented with numbers rather than percentages, then in many ways you haven't got as much information as if you had it the other way round. Look at the following example:

The number of people in the UK who are classified as obese has increased over the past ten years. More than eight million people in the country fall into this category. However the number of obese people varies from area to area. A few examples will show this.

South East London	*54,144*
Avon, Gloucestershire, and Wiltshire	*60,896*
Shropshire and Staffordshire	*72,135*
Surrey and Sussex	*72,160*
Co. Durham and Tees Valley	*78,624*

Because the problem of obesity varies so much from area to area, the Government needs to concentrate its campaign to try to solve the problem in those areas that have the biggest problem.

Faced with these figures, we would think that the argument should encourage the Government to focus its campaign in, say, the last three places on the list rather than the first two. But raw numbers like these can give us limited information. What do we need to know about the figures to see if this is what the Government should do?

We need to know what the figures mean in terms of the population in these different areas. For example, is the figure of 54,144 for South East London a bigger or smaller proportion of the population than the 60,896 for Avon, Gloucestershire, and Wiltshire?

This is where percentages would be very helpful. Look at the same information presented as percentages of the population that are obese in each area.

South East London	*19.2*
Avon, Gloucestershire, and Wiltshire	*17.3*
Shropshire and Staffordshire	*22.9*
Surrey and Sussex	*17.6*
Co. Durham and Tees Valley	*27.3*

Now the picture looks rather different. Though Co. Durham and the Tees Valley remain in the same position in the table in terms of the seriousness of the problem of obesity, Surrey and Sussex have now to be seen very differently. Their relatively large population meant that their obesity figure was likely to be high, even though the percentage of people who are obese is relatively low.

Sometimes, however, we do need to know the numbers in order to judge the significance of a percentage. This is when we are given figures on a percentage increase or decrease.

It is often reported that teenagers are getting so obsessed with their appearance that they are prepared to use cosmetic surgery, even as young as 16. However, if we look at figures from the US, we find that fewer teenagers (those aged 18 or younger) than before are having cosmetic surgery. In 2001 3.5 per cent of all cosmetic surgery procedures were carried out on teenagers. In 2002, the percentage was 3.2, and in 2003 it had gone right down to 2.7. This shows that fewer and fewer teenagers in the US are worrying about their body image.

The conclusion of this argument is that fewer teenagers in the US are worrying about their body image. The word 'fewer' is being used in terms of numbers, but the evidence is presented in terms of percentages. In order to judge whether the percentages are enough for the author to draw their conclusion, we need to know the numbers. These are the numbers for teenagers (18 or younger) having cosmetic surgery procedures.

2001   298,700 procedures
2002   220,077
2003   223,594

As you can see, the picture is slightly less straightforward when we look at the numbers. The conclusion about fewer teenagers worrying about their body image is less easy to draw, given the numerical increase in teenagers having cosmetic surgery in 2003 compared to 2002. In this case, the number that was particularly relevant was the total number from which the percentage was taken.

This example highlighted the importance of knowing what a percentage refers to when we are evaluating evidence. In this case, the percentages were of the number of teenagers in the total number of cosmetic surgery procedures, not of the total number of teenagers having cosmetic surgery. Because the total number of cosmetic procedures is affected much more by what adults are doing, rather than teenagers, our evaluation of the evidence benefited from knowing the numbers involved.

What we have seen is that, though percentages normally tell us more than raw numbers, there are times when the author's use of a percentage might not tell us enough. In such cases, the numbers can often tell us more. For example, the statistic that cosmetic surgery for teenagers grew by 562 per cent between 1994 and 2001 needs to be evaluated in the light of what the numbers in 1994 were. Thus, if they were very low, then a large percentage increase doesn't mean that the numbers themselves grew hugely.

RATES

You will sometimes see evidence presented as a rate. This is often as a 'rate per 1000', but can be per 10,000, per 100,000, or more. It can even be a rate per one thing. An example of this last one is what is called the fertility rate. This shows the average number of children per woman in different countries.

Niger	*8.0*
Mali	*7.0*
Malawi	*6.10*
Bhutan	*5.02*
UK	*1.60*
Italy	*1.23*
Hong Kong	*1.00*

This type of rate is useful because it gives a simple way of looking at something.

A percentage is, of course, a rate per 100, but not all rates per 100 are percentages. A percentage is the proportion of something within a group; a rate per 100 compares one thing to another. For example, the numbers of men and women in a population are sometimes given in this way. This is because it is a better way of expressing the proportion of men compared to that of women.

The number of men in a population per 100 women	
UK	*95*
US	*97*
France	*95*
Australia	*99*
Nigeria	*101*
China	*106*
India	*106*
Pakistan	*105*
United Arab Emirates	*190*

(You might want to consider explanations for these differences.)

A rate that is often expressed as a figure per thousand is the birth rate. This is to give a way of showing the number of births in a country as a proportion of the population, so that we can compare the number of births between countries.

Average number of live births per 1000 population, 2000–2005
Niger	*55.2*
Rwanda	*44.0*
Pakistan	*35.9*
France	*12.8*
UK	*11.0*
Japan	*9.2*
Germany	*8.7*

Not surprisingly, for the same reason as birth rates, death rates are normally expressed per 1000. An interesting set of figures that could usefully be read in conjunction with the table on live births is that of infant mortality. This is expressed as the number of deaths of infants up to their first birthday per 1000 live births (rather than per 1000 population).

Number of deaths per 1000 live births, 2000–2005
Niger	*125.7*
Rwanda	*115.5*
Pakistan	*86.5*
UK	*5.4*
France	*5.0*
Germany	*4.5*
Japan	*3.2*

You could look at the two sets of figures on births and infant mortality and consider what, if any, relationship there could be between the two.

Whenever you see a figure expressed as a rate, whatever evaluation you do with it, you will see that saying 'it doesn't take into account the size of the population' is wrong. It's wrong because that's precisely what it does do. Thus, if we look at the international figures for serious assault and for theft, we might be surprised at the country that heads the league table. This is Australia which had 737 serious assaults per 100,000 population and 6,653 thefts per 100,000 population. Why these figures are the highest in the world is something to consider, but you will obviously want to think about how the figures are collected, and how the terms 'serious assault' and 'theft' are defined in different countries. But, whatever evaluation you do of these figures, references to the size of the population aren't going to be relevant.

Sometimes, numbers could be much more usefully expressed as rates in relation to population. For example, league tables of scientific or sporting achievement take no account of the size of the population. For example, one measure of a country's scientific achievement is the number of Nobel Prizes that its scientists get (a sort of Olympics of scientific achievement).

Nobel Prizes for science (including economics) 1901–2002

US	*159*
UK	*70*
Germany	*46*
France	*21*

This table shows the top four places in the league table. It shows the US as completely dominating it. However, look at the next table showing these countries in the same order, but this time showing the size of population (given in millions).

US	*288.5*
UK	*59.7*
Germany	*82.0*
France	*59.7*

If you compare the two tables, you can see that, if we were to express Nobel Prizes in terms of population size, then the country with the most impressive performance is the UK. Well done! What about the performances of Germany and France?

INDICES

You won't often come across these but sometimes evidence is presented in the form of what is called an index. The word is used to mean a 'measure'. It's a way of comparing different examples of the same thing against one measure (a bit like comparing the size of different things using a ruler).

An index normally takes the figure of 100.00 as representing something that countries, cities, or whatever are compared to. This means that a 'score' of less or more than 100 can tell us something about the things that are being compared.

One such index is what is called the Human Development Index. This is a measure produced by the United Nations that combines things like income levels, life expectancy, average years of schooling, and literacy to give an index of the quality of life in different countries. If we take 100.00 to represent a level that would have a very high combined score of all of the things in the index, then we can compare countries' quality of life. The country with the highest index is Norway with a score of 94.4; the country with the lowest score is Sierra Leone with 27.5. (The UK comes in at 11th = with 93.0.) As you can see, this quality of life index doesn't have to be compared to size of population. It is just compared to the figure of 100.00.

Another index does the same thing with the quality of life of different cities. This time, the 100.00 figure is taken to be New York. This city is taken as the measure by which all other cities can be compared, using such factors as the facilities available to the residents, like transport and education, quality and availability of food, climate, and levels of personal safety. There are thirty-eight cities that exceed the 100.00 set by the quality of life in New York.

The two top ones are both in Switzerland (Zurich and Geneva, both with a score of 106.5). The lowest is Baghdad with 14.5. (London is 35th = with a score of 100.5.)

TIMESCALES

Evidence will often be presented that shows change over a given timescale. For example, we had an argument earlier in which the author used figures showing a decline in the percentage of teenagers having cosmetic surgery.

> *It is often reported that teenagers are getting so obsessed with their appearance that they are prepared to use cosmetic surgery, even as young as 16. However, if we look at figures from the US, we find that fewer teenagers (those aged 18 or younger) than before are having cosmetic surgery. In 2001 3.5 per cent of all cosmetic surgery procedures were carried out on teenagers. In 2002, the percentage was 3.2, and in 2003 it had gone right down to 2.7. This shows that fewer and fewer teenagers in the US are worrying about their body image.*

We have already done some evaluation of the author's evidence that showed that the percentages hid the significance of the numbers involved. There is another way in which the significance of evidence, of whatever sort, can be changed. If we look again at the evidence on teenagers having cosmetic surgery, we see that the timescale is 2001-2003. Using this timescale, the author was able to show an uninterrupted decline in the percentage, a decline that they used in order to draw their conclusion. However, what happens if we extend the timescale a little? If we look back to 1997, the picture becomes much less clear.

Percentage of total cosmetic surgery procedures carried out on those who were 18 years-old or younger

1997	*2.9*
1998	*1.3*
1999	*3.8*
2000	*2.5*
2001	*3.5*
2002	*3.2*
2003	*2.7*

These figures give a rather different picture. Instead of one that shows a steady decline in teenage cosmetic surgery, we see that the starting point in the original argument of 2001 distorted the significance of the figures. The 2001 figure was an unusually high percentage, so any decline from it could be seen more as returning to a normal position rather than a decline that was significant.

Thus, when you're evaluating some evidence which involves a timescale, consider whether the timescale that the author is using might distort the significance of the evidence.

An author might use timescales to argue that one thing has caused another. In other words, if they can show that what was happening during one timescale was also happening (or not happening) during another, then they can claim that they have found an explanation. An example shows this.

There has been an increase in the number of fatal road accidents in the UK since 1993. If we are looking for an explanation for this increase, we need to look at something else that has happened since 1993. Some people have argued that the use of mobile phones whilst driving is the cause. But the first mobile phones appeared in 1985, and so the timescale doesn't fit at all. What does fit this timescale is the introduction of speed cameras. There is evidence that speed cameras actually cause accidents. For example, in one county in England (Hertfordshire), between 2003 and 2004 there was a 24 per cent increase in speed cameras, and a 34 per cent increase in road deaths during the same period. It is clear that speed cameras should never be used on our roads.

The author is doing a lot of work with evidence here. But the evidence on timescales is a central part of their argument. The author is looking for an explanation of why road deaths in this country have increased since 1993. They look at two such explanations: mobile phones and speed cameras. The first is dismissed on the grounds that it doesn't fit the timescale. The author is right that mobile phones were introduced in 1985, but they have used this information without considering whether the timescale of *usage* of mobile phones is the same as the one that starts when they were introduced. So, what do we find when we look at the figures for mobile phone users from 1985?

We find something very interesting. The number of mobile phone users stayed very, very low in the UK from 1985 until one year in particular. That year was 1993. Since then, the number of mobile phone users in the UK has shot up to over 50 million. So mobile phones do fit the timescale after all. Of course, though we've done some very important evaluation of the author's use of evidence, we haven't shown that, therefore, the increased use of mobile phones whilst driving caused the increase in road deaths. (Just as the author hasn't shown that they haven't been at least part of the explanation.) Look at the section on *post hoc* arguments, beginning on page 94, for more discussion of this subject of using evidence to show that one thing causes another.

Before you leave the passage on speed cameras, there's another thing to note. We found that the timescale for usage of mobile phones fitted the author's timescale for road deaths very well. But it was the exact way in which it did that was important. What if we had said to the author of the argument something like 'but you're not taking into account the fact that in recent years more people are using mobile phones'? They could have said, 'Yes, I know, but I'm looking at a very specific timescale, that of 1993 onwards, so your reference to "recent years" is too vague'. And they'd be right. Whenever we're trying to do some evaluation with timescales, then we must be careful to be very specific. A timescale of 1993 to the present needs to be dealt with as something as specific as that, not vaguely as in 'recent years' or even more vaguely as 'more people now use mobile phones'. Vagueness is something that you leave at the door when you do Critical Thinking. Precision is something you carry with you at all times. Please.

USING UNUSUALLY-PRESENTED EVIDENCE

Sometimes an author will present evidence in a way that is unusual. But it can be an effective way of presenting it.

Look at two different ways of presenting evidence on the number of cars abandoned in England in 2004.

In 2004, 221,424 cars were abandoned in England. This is because it costs people to dispose of their cars, rather than being able to sell them for scrap, as they used to. The solution would be to make the car manufacturers pay for the disposal of unwanted cars. After all, they made the cars in the first place. The Government should bring in a law to enforce this.

If all the cars that had been abandoned in England in 2004 were put in a line, they would stretch all the way from London to Berlin. As the crow flies, that's 578 miles. So as you travel along mile after mile of unwanted, broken-down, rusty cars, it is clear that something has to change. Disposing of cars these days costs people money, rather than being able to sell them for scrap, as they used to. The solution would be to make the car manufacturers pay for the disposal of unwanted cars. After all, they made the cars in the first place. The Government should bring in a law to enforce this.

Though the two pieces of evidence are the same, the second way of presenting it is unusual in trying to create some sort of image. You'll find other examples, using the capacity of football grounds as the measure. In the end, of course, however the evidence is presented, its significance has to be evaluated in terms of how it supports the author's argument.

GENERALISING FROM EVIDENCE

What do we mean by **generalising** from evidence? Very simply, that an author will take a particular piece of evidence about one thing and apply it to other things. This can mean applying evidence of one thing to a different time, to a different group, to a different event, and so on. In many ways, using evidence often requires generalisation. An author will be saying that, if A has happened in this situation, then A will happen in others. Therefore we can draw a conclusion about A from this piece of evidence on it. Is there a problem with this?

In Critical Thinking we often hear that there are problems in generalising from evidence. We need therefore to look at what these problems are and when we're likely to find them. It is too simple to say that an author shouldn't generalise. There are sometimes very good reasons for why we can generalise from evidence. For example, if today you were to take a sample of opinions on something amongst your fellow-students, you would feel entirely justified in generalising from the results of that sample to their opinions in two weeks' time. If you didn't, this is only because you'd know that something had happened to change these opinions. We are always happy to generalise from one thing to another, from one time to another, from one group to another, unless we're aware of something that would make us unhappy to do this.

As a result, we should extend the same tolerance of generalisation to other people. And, in extending the same tolerance, we need to think about situations in which an author is wrong to generalise. Look at the next example.

> *We tend to think that there's not much we can do to stop the growth of illegal drugs. After all, the experience of the US in the 1920s when the sale of alcohol was banned (called Prohibition) has shown us that people who want a banned product will manage to get it somehow. But there is another lesson from history that can be learned. In the nineteenth century, parts of Britain had massive problems of opium addiction. This was particularly the case in the Fens, a rather desolate part of Cambridgeshire. By a combination of restricting the supply of opium and heavily discouraging people from taking it, opium-taking in Britain had almost completely disappeared by the end of the nineteenth century. Thus we should tackle the present problem of illegal drugs in the same aggressive way.*

In this argument, the author has made two generalisations. The first is using the US experience of Prohibition to show that 'people who want a banned product will manage to get it'. The second is to take the British experience of solving the problem of opium addiction in order to show that the present problem of illegal drugs can be solved. Are either or both of these generalisations acceptable?

The first thing you'll probably have noticed is that they contradict each other. The evidence on Prohibition is used to show that we can't stop people getting banned things; the evidence on dealing with the opium problem in Britain is used to show that we can.

Apart from this contradiction (which is, of course, a serious problem for the argument), is the author right to generalise? In order to answer this question, we must ask a general one which must be used in all evaluations of evidence involving generalisation.

• How similar are the two things?

In each case, the question should be specified in particular terms. In this one, these give us the following questions.

Prohibition

• Was the situation in the US in the 1920s sufficiently similar to that of present-day UK to be relevant?

- Is the experience of the banning of alcohol sufficiently similar to that of banning illegal drugs?

Opium

- Was the problem of opium-taking in the nineteenth century in Britain sufficiently similar to that of illegal drugs in the UK today?

- Is the taking of opium sufficiently similar to the taking of today's illegal drugs?

As we can see, acceptable generalisation of evidence requires that we use the test of *sufficient similarity*. Is the first thing sufficiently similar to the second (and any others) to enable us to say that the first is a reliable guide to the second (and others)? If it is, then the author is entitled to generalise. If it isn't, then they're not.

Another way of looking at this issue is to distinguish between 'generalisation' and 'over-generalisation'. When an author over-generalises, they have failed the test of sufficient similarity. They have taken the evidence to have more in it that it allows.

> *Monarch butterflies have been used to test whether or not genetically-modified (GM) crops are a danger to our health. In a famous study, GM maize pollen was dusted on to the leaves of milkweed, the main source of food for these butterflies. Half of them died, and the rest grew to only 50 per cent of their normal size. Given that monarch butterflies live only for a very short time, this is very worrying that the GM pollen could have such an effect so quickly. The implications for us are disturbing. We are likely to be exposed to the problems of GM for years, with the bad effects on our health building up to create massive problems for us. The monarch butterfly is often called the 'Bambi of insects'. Given the evidence of what GM does to Bambi, we should ban all GM crops now.*

In this argument, the author moves from monarch butterflies to humans in one go. They take the study of these butterflies eating GM pollen on milkweed to be *sufficiently similar* to our experience that they can conclude that we should ban GM crops to protect our health. In order to consider whether this is over-generalisation, you would need to consider this issue of sufficient similarity.

- Can the study of monarch butterflies be generalised to anything else? For example, can it be generalised to other insects? Can it be generalised beyond insects to, say, mammals? Most importantly for this argument, can it be generalised directly to humans (as the author does)?

- Can one study of the effect of GM crops be generalised at all? Would we need other studies of the same insect to be able to say that GM crops are a problem for monarch butterflies?

- Can a study of an insect that eats one food be generalised to other species that might eat a wide variety of foods?

Looking at these questions, you would probably judge that the evidence had been over-generalised in that it failed to pass the test of sufficient similarity. What about the next argument?

The success of yoga in the treatment of various conditions is increasingly being recognised. A good example is asthma. In a recent study, asthma patients were divided into two groups. One group was given a programme of yoga, and the other was given a programme of relaxation exercises. The results were that, compared to the relaxation group, the yoga group showed much lower sensitivity to substances such as pollen or dust, a key feature of asthma. The yoga group also reported a greater reduction in tiredness. In consequence, people with asthma should be advised to take up yoga.

The test of sufficient similarity produces the following question.

- Is this study of asthma patients sufficient for the author's conclusion that people with asthma should be advised to take up yoga?

Answers to that question would want to look at the issue of whether this study has done enough to prove that yoga is something that can benefit people who suffer from asthma. It could be said, for example, that the study compared only yoga with relaxation exercises. In consequence, the conclusion could be said to be overdrawn in that the author hasn't obviously considered other treatments that might be even more effective than yoga. However, the use of the evidence is much less of a problem than in the monarch butterflies argument. One study of asthma patients does probably have relevance to the treatment of asthma. One study of monarch butterflies is less happily generalised to humans.

ACTIVITY 6

The following argument uses lots of different evidence to support its conclusion. Identify the conclusion, and then assess the evidence to see how far it supports this conclusion.

People who drive 4x4 cars or people carriers should pay a much higher rate of road tax (perhaps at least three times as much) than people who drive other cars. There are many reasons for why this should happen. When a 4x4 collides with a small car, people in the smaller car are twelve times as likely to be killed in such a collision as people in the 4x4. People carriers and 4x4s are normally twice as heavy as small cars, and 4x4s have high bumpers that can hit a small car above the level of any side-protection system they might have. The whole problem of these cars is made worse when we see that there has been an increase in their sales. In 1994, sales of 4x4s and people carriers were 4.5 per cent of total car sales; in 2004, such sales had gone up to 11.9 per cent. The significance of these figures is emphasised when we look at what's happened to the sales of small cars. These have gone up from 26 per cent of car sales in 1994 to 35 per cent of car sales in 2004. This increase in the sales of small cars, 4x4s, and people carriers results each year in at least twenty more deaths and cases of very serious injury among drivers of small cars. In 2004, 179,000 4x4s were sold compared with 126,000 people carriers. However, the 4x4 figure was about double that of 1994, whereas the figure for people carriers was ten times the 1994 figure.

ACTIVITY 7

Some additional evidence is provided here. Take each piece of evidence and decide whether, if it is true, it would strengthen or weaken the author's argument.

(A) The safety of cars in relation to pedestrians is measured on a scale from no stars to three (with three being the best). The larger 4x4s perform very badly in pedestrian crash protection tests. Only one of them received more than one star; one of them received none. Most family cars are awarded at least two stars, and many have achieved three.

(B) 4x4 cars produce more environmental pollution than most cars. For example, one of them produces twice the amount of carbon dioxide per kilometre than a Ford Mondeo (an ordinary family car).

(C) 4x4s are 25 per cent more likely to be involved in accidents than ordinary family cars.

(D) At least 20 per cent of 4x4s are bought in Greater London. 4x4s are sometimes called 'off-road' cars because they can be driven across land such as fields, unlike ordinary cars.

(E) Evidence from the US shows that someone hit by a 4x4 has twice the risk of being killed by it as someone hit by an ordinary family car travelling at the same speed.

ACTIVITY 6: COMMENTARY

The conclusion of the argument is the first sentence.

The first piece of evidence is the third sentence:

When a 4x4 collides with a small car, people in the smaller car are twelve times as likely to be killed in such a collision as people in the 4x4.

This is explained by the evidence in the next sentence.

People carriers and 4x4s are normally twice as heavy as small cars, and 4x4s have high bumpers that can hit a small car above the level of any side-protection system they might have.

What sort of evaluation can we make of this evidence and the explanation for it?

* Without the explanation, we might have responded that we would expect small cars to be more vulnerable in an accident with a larger car, simply because they are small. In this way, the evidence does not in itself show that 4x4s are the problem. Though, given the explanation, we can see that 4x4s might be a particular problem, the evidence doesn't include reference to people carriers.

* This last point is important. The author's conclusion puts 4x4s and people carriers in the same category, but some of the evidence refers to 4x4s only.

* The first piece of evidence does not tell us anything about the frequency of accidents involving 4x4s and small cars. Though the evidence points to a greater risk for people in small cars in such accidents, it tells us nothing about whether or not such accidents are more or less frequent than other accidents. For example, it could be that 4x4s have a number of safety features designed to reduce the chances of them causing accidents.

* The explanation regarding weight of the vehicle provides very relevant information on why 4x4s and people carriers could increase the risk of injury for people in smaller cars in an accident. The same information might, of course, be used with regard to medium- and large-sized cars. Perhaps a lot of vehicles are significantly heavier than small cars. In addition, as discussed above, the evidence on the higher risk for people in small cars has been presented only in terms of 4x4 cars.

* The explanation in terms of the high bumpers of 4x4s is particularly relevant to the

evidence regarding the greater risk of people in small cars. However, it does not relate to people carriers.

The next line of argument is concerned with sales of the different types of cars.

The whole problem of these cars is made worse when we see that there has been an increase in their sales. In 1994, sales of 4x4s and people carriers were 4.5 per cent of total car sales; in 2004, such sales had gone up to 11.9 per cent.

- The percentages given refer to those of total sales. Given this, it is not necessarily the case that the actual numbers of 4x4s and people carriers have gone up. For them to have done so, sales of all types of vehicles would need to have increased. Though you would take this to be almost certainly true, it is worth making the point that the percentages themselves don't tell us this.

- Of course, the author is developing a different point. This is that the proportion of 4x4s and people carriers of the total number of vehicles has gone up. Given the evidence on their problems for small cars, this is meant to be significant.

- The evidence on percentages of sales in 1994 and 2004 does not show the different percentages for 4x4s and people carriers. Given the extra evidence on the particular problems of 4x4s (as, apparently, opposed to people carriers), we need to know how this percentage increase in sales is distributed between the two types of car.

- If we think of timescales, we can't tell from the 1994 and 2004 evidence whether or not 11.9 per cent (the 2004 figure) represents a continuing increase, or whether the figure had been higher in, say, 2002 and/or 2003. Similarly, we don't know from the evidence whether or not the 1994 figure was unusually low.

The significance of these figures is emphasised when we look at what's happened to the sales of small cars. These have gone up from 26 per cent of car sales in 1994 to 35 per cent of car sales in 2004.

- We could make the same point as above with regard to the significance of the percentage increase in sales. Percentage increases of total sales do not in themselves tell us that there are more small cars. Again, though we would probably accept that total sales have gone up, this piece of evidence does not tell this.

- There is an interesting point of definition here. How is 'small' car being defined? Are there no 'small' 4x4s?

- If you add together the two percentages given for sales of 4x4s, people carriers, and small cars, this comes to 46.9 per cent. As a result, we can see that a majority (small, but still a majority) of cars falls outside these categories. Most cars then are medium-sized or large. In that the author gives us no information on these in relation to accidents, weight, and safety aspects, it is difficult to judge whether or not 4x4s and people carriers are more of a problem than these other cars. If they are more of a problem, it is difficult to judge how much more.

This increase in the sales of small cars, 4x4s, and people carriers results each year in at least twenty more deaths and cases of very serious injury among drivers of small cars.

- An obvious response to this statistic is 'how is it calculated?' One of the key words is 'results'. This indicates that the author is referring to actual accidents rather than predictions. The word 'more' is another very significant one. It indicates that the author believes that, if the percentages of these three types of cars were not as they are, then there have been accidents that wouldn't have happened. Of course, a problem with this sort of evidence is that we don't know for sure what would have happened if things had been different. Perhaps there would have been more accidents between small cars, or more between large and small cars.

- Here we don't have evidence given as a percentage, but as a number. Because of this, we don't know whether 'at least twenty more' is significant. Given the evidence on increases in sales of 4x4s, people carriers, and small cars, would we have expected this number to be higher or lower? In addition, given the evidence (that we calculated) that the majority of cars fall outside these three categories, what is the significance of this for the number of accidents? Would a reduction in the sales of medium-sized and large cars be good news if many of these were replaced by small cars?

In 2004, 179,000 4x4s were sold compared with 126,000 people carriers. However, the 4x4 figure was about double that of 1994, whereas the figure for people carriers was ten times the 1994 figure.

- This evidence has two parts to it. We are given numbers of sales of 4x4s and people carriers in 2004. We are also given information on the rate of increase of these sales. At one level, given the previous evidence on the specific dangers of 4x4s, the author should be pleased that the rate of increase in sales of people carriers is much greater than that of 4x4s. However, given that the argument largely lumps the two types together (as in the previous evidence), this information is pretty well neutral in the argument. It neither strengthens nor weakens the argument.

- The evidence does illustrate something useful. We had looked earlier about the significance of a baseline figure when we have to judge the significance of increases or decreases in something. Here we're told that the sale of 179,000 4x4s in 2004 is about twice that of sales in 1994 and that the sale of 126,000 people carriers is ten times the figure for 1994. We can work out from these numbers what the baseline figures would have been (approximately). Sales of 4x4s must have been about 89,500 in 1994, and those of people carriers about 12,600. What these figures remind us is how baseline figures can enable us to judge evidence such as 'ten times the number'. In this case, given the high baseline figure for 4x4s, and the relatively low one for people carriers, we wouldn't have expected the 4x4 increase to be anything like as large as that for people carriers. Watch out for this happening in evidence.

So, was the argument a good one? Was the conclusion well-supported by the evidence?

- The first thing that you probably saw was that the conclusion has a very specific focus. It's not something like 'We should make 4x4 and people carrier manufacturers redesign their vehicles to make them safer'. This would certainly fit with the sort of evidence presented.

- However, the conclusion is that drivers of these vehicles should pay more road tax than people who drive other cars. Does the evidence support this conclusion? Only if we make one or both of the following assumptions:

  making these car-owners pay more road tax would deter them (or enough of them) from having such vehicles;

  the extra money could be used in some way to deal with the costs of the extra casualties of accidents.

  Without either or both of these assumptions, the conclusion doesn't fit well with the evidence.

- On balance, we can say that some of the evidence was relevant to the conclusion (with the assumptions slotted in), but some (especially the last piece) was not obviously relevant.

ACTIVITY 7: COMMENTARY

One general point you can make about each of the pieces of evidence is that the author's argument was about both 4x4s and people carriers. All of the evidence you were given refers only to 4x4s. In this way, if any of the evidence does strengthen the argument, it will do so only in relation to that part of the argument.

(A) brings in more evidence about safety. The author had used evidence showing the problem of 4x4s and people carriers in relation to accidents with small cars. This was used to draw the conclusion that such cars should have higher road taxes. If the problem of increased risk of injury in accidents between small cars and 4x4s is used as part of the argument, then further evidence of the increased risk of injury from 4x4s in accidents with pedestrians must have some relevance. However, the evidence refers only to the 'larger 4x4s', so it has both a strength and a weakness.

(B) provides evidence on something that the author hadn't considered in their argument. The author's conclusion was based entirely on the issue of risk of injury in accidents. So how relevant might information on pollution be? It depends how you see the argument. If you see it as being no more than an argument using risks of injury in accidents to support a conclusion that is concerned with increasing road tax (for whatever purpose), then you are likely to see this as irrelevant. However, if you see the higher levels of pollution from 4x4s as giving another reason to get their drivers to be deterred from having one or being made to pay 'compensation' to the rest of us, then it is relevant. It certainly fits with the conclusion, and could be seen as making it stronger.

(C) This is very strong evidence. It actually answers a query we raised when we were looking at the evidence in the passage. We considered there that, though the evidence indicated a higher risk of injury from 4x4 cars for people in small cars, we didn't know if 4x4s were involved in proportionally fewer accidents. This evidence very strongly deals with that query. This significantly higher accident rate combines with the evidence in the passage to make a much stronger argument.

(D) This is an interesting one. Many of the complaints about 4x4s are that people who have them don't need a vehicle that can drive across muddy fields. They use them simply for driving around towns and cities, hence the frequent nickname, the 'Chelsea tractor' (given emphasis by lots of middle class mothers driving their children to school in them). The only way you could see this evidence as strengthening the argument is to stress that, because people don't need this sort of vehicle for towns and cities, they should be made to pay for the problems 4x4s cause. (But what about those people who do use them for driving across muddy fields?)

(E) This strengthens the argument along the same lines as (A). However, it is stronger than (A) in that it doesn't have the problem of referring only to 'larger 4x4s'. If (E) is true, then it provides further evidence on the safety problems of 4x4s, and so strengthens the conclusion.

NB. You were asked to consider the significance of this additional evidence if it were true. It needs to be stressed that all of the evidence is true in the sense that it reports evidence that has been published. None of it was made up.

EVALUATING ARGUMENTS

LOOKING FOR STRENGTHS IN ARGUMENTS

The task of evaluating arguments returns us to the idea of whether or not a conclusion of an argument is overdrawn. You will remember that a conclusion is overdrawn if there is not enough in the reasoning to support it. To some extent, most arguments you'll meet in Critical Thinking could be seen as overdrawn in some way. This is because the reasons, at most, give no more than strong support for the conclusion. A different conclusion could still possibly be drawn.

In the next example, the conclusion that is drawn is in a way demanded by the reasons.

> *The 16.27 train to London is 30 minutes late. If the 16.27 is more than 20 minutes late, then passengers will miss the connection to Cambridge. Therefore passengers on the 16.27 to London will miss the connection to Cambridge.*

The conclusion of this argument looks anything but overdrawn. The force of the reasons acting together requires this conclusion to be drawn. (Although it works only by assuming that the connection to Cambridge will not itself be delayed.)

The next example does something different.

> *Over the past month, the 16.27 to London has very often been more than 30 minutes late. If the 16.27 is more than 20 minutes late, then passengers miss the connection to Cambridge. Therefore passengers on today's 16.27 will miss the connection to Cambridge.*

The conclusion of this argument is clearly overdrawn. In that we don't know if today's 16.27 is typical of the late ones, we cannot conclude anything as definite as the author does. So how do we fit the conclusion with the reasons to make it fit, to make it, at the very least, much less overdrawn?

The next example does this.

> *Over the past month, the 16.27 to London has very often been more than 30 minutes late. If the 16.27 is more than 20 minutes late, then passengers miss the connection to Cambridge. Therefore, if today's 16.27 is like those that have often been late, passengers will miss the connection to Cambridge.*

As you can see, we have made the argument very strong by restricting the scope of the conclusion, by weakening it. We can also make an argument stronger by strengthening the reasons.

Look at the next example.

> *Each year 100,000 albatrosses (large sea birds) are killed by fishing boats. The lines that boats use can stretch for fifty miles and the birds get caught in them whilst searching for fish for their young. Having got caught in the lines, the albatrosses are pulled under the water and drowned. Their chicks, sitting in a nest possibly hundreds of miles away, will wait in vain for their parents to return. Since the parents never will, the chicks will die from starvation.*

What conclusion fits this passage?

(A)   The fishing lines that kill albatrosses should be banned.

(B)   The fishing lines that kill albatrosses should be rarely used.

(C)   The fishing lines that kill albatrosses should be used only in areas where albatrosses rarely go.

Testing these possible conclusions against the information given in the passage will require that we make some assumptions clear.

All of the possible conclusions require that we assume that the loss of so many albatrosses is something unacceptable. This could be seen in terms of the birds being an endangered species, and that their decline or even disappearance is of great concern to us.

It can be seen that all of the three possible conclusions could be drawn. (A), being the strongest, takes most out of the evidence provided in the passage. (C), being a little weaker than (B), takes the least out. What happens if we add some more evidence?

The fishing lines also kill many other species of seabird.

This extra piece of evidence now makes (C) rather too weak, in that (C) restricts itself to trying to solve the problem regarding albatrosses. On the other hand, both (A) and (B) have been strengthened. We could add some more evidence.

If the numbers of albatrosses go really low, then they will never recover, whatever we do to try to help them. They will leave an important gap in the eco-system that can never be filled. The same thing happened to cod, which was so over-fished off the eastern coast of the US, that even when cod fishing was banned, the fish could never re-establish itself.

This extra evidence makes (B) much less overdrawn. What would make (B) even more defendable as a conclusion would be if we had evidence that the 100,000 albatrosses lost each year by fishing lines, together with the consequent death of albatross chicks through starvation, was a very high proportion of the albatross species. Without knowing this information, it is difficult to judge the significance of the figures.

The same thing could be said about (A). The extra evidence on their possible disappearance from the eco-system gives strength to the recommendation that the fishing lines should be banned.

What we have seen is that when we are evaluating arguments, we are doing no more than looking at the extent to which the reasons support the conclusion. It might be that we have to consider the significance of particular evidence or examples, but in the end an evaluation of the argument is what is being asked for. Is it a good one or not? Is it good in parts, and much less so in others?

LOOKING FOR WEAKNESSES IN ARGUMENTS

When we are evaluating arguments, there are certain types of weakness in arguments that actually have their own names. The names do no more than describe what the weakness in the argument is. You don't need to remember or to use the names, but they can be useful reminders of the different types of weakness. They're also a useful 'shorthand' way of describing a weakness. We begin with a very familiar weakness: it has the Latin name *post hoc*.

POST HOC

Post hoc (pronounced 'post' as in 'letters' and 'hoc' rhyming with 'sock'). The full Latin name of this weakness is *post hoc ergo propter hoc*. This full name makes it very clear what's going, because it means 'After this, therefore because of this'. In other words, if one thing (say, you catching a cold) happened after another (say, your friend sneezing near you), then your cold was caused by your friend's sneezing.

Arguments very often rely on what are taken to be links between pieces of evidence to support their conclusion. In many cases, of course, the author might well be right. You will be able to think of many examples where one thing follows another because it was caused by the other.

Emma's alarm clock didn't go off. Emma was late for school.

Very heavy snow fell all night. Traffic was very slow-moving in the morning.

Ben took paracetamol for his headache. Ben's headache went half an hour later.

In each of these cases, it doesn't seem difficult to see that the first event is very likely to have caused the second. Though we could think of alternative explanations for each of the second events, we are not going to be surprised by the suggestion that, in each case, the first caused the second.

What about the next example?

The total distance travelled by motorbikes or scooters increased by 10.4% in 2003. The number of motorcyclists (including those riding scooters) killed increased by 14% in 2003.

Could it be said that, in this example, the second event was caused by the first? It wouldn't be ridiculous to see a causal connection between the two, but it's not as straightforward as in the first group of examples. It's not as straightforward because we could think of plenty of other possible explanations for why the number of motorcyclists killed increased in 2003.

- Perhaps the number of young (inexperienced) motorcyclists increased in 2003.

- Perhaps the number of cars on the road increased in that year, making motorcycling more dangerous (simply with more traffic being about).

- Perhaps the number of motorcyclists killed in 2002 was unusually low, so making the 14% increase less significant.

What can we say about the next example?

The number of people seeking political asylum in the UK went down by 33% in 2004. The number of people seeking political asylum in France went up by 3% in 2004.

One obvious point can be made. Even if there is a causal link between the two, it is in no way clear what the link is.

- Did the UK's reduction in the percentage applying for political asylum cause the increase in the percentage applying to France?
- Did the increase in the percentage applying to France for political asylum cause the decline in the UK figure?
- Is the causal link a combination of the two previous points?
- Is there no connection between the two pieces of evidence?
- Is there a third factor which explains both (for example, was there something happening in another country which itself caused the different figures?)?

As we can see, the relationship between pieces of evidence needs to be looked at critically. When an argument takes two things/events/statistics as being related such that one caused the other, then we need to look to see if this is likely.

We can use four ways to evaluate the relationship between the two events. These are

- Looking for different explanations
- Only part of the cause
- Only coincidence
- Simple causation

To show how these can be applied to an example, look at the next one.

The sales of ice cream in the seaside town of Bournemouth increase every summer. The number of car accidents in Bournemouth also increase every summer. Therefore, to reduce the number of car accidents, we should restrict the sales of ice cream.

You should be able to see that, though the two pieces of evidence are true, there are clear problems with the conclusion. Of course, the idea of a causal relationship between the two pieces of evidence isn't utterly without something to it. We might, for example, argue that, because in the summer people have a greater likelihood of driving with an ice cream in their hand, they have a higher risk of a causing an accident.

- But there is a simpler (and more likely) explanation. This is that the two pieces of evidence are linked, but not in a causal way. In the summer, lots more people drive to the seaside (including Bournemouth) and lots more people buy ice creams at the seaside (including Bournemouth). As a result, we would expect more car accidents for the reason there are more cars.

  The increase in ice cream sales is correlated with the increase in car accidents but does not cause it. You'll sometimes see *post hoc* arguments being evaluated in terms of 'correlation but not cause'. What is meant by this is that two things (number, percentage, etc.) can go in the same direction (increase or decrease), but they are not linked in a causal relationship. Things can also go in a different direction and be seen as correlated. For example, the number of car journeys could have gone up in a year, and the number of rail passengers could have gone down in the same year. The two things are correlated but whether or not the first caused the second is to be examined. There might be another explanation.

- Though two things correlate, the link between the two could be explained only partially causally. With our example of Bournemouth, the increase in the sales of ice creams could explain a small part of the increase in the number of car accidents (using our scenario of people driving with inadequate care as they concentrate on their mint chocolate chip rather than the road).

- Of course, the two things could have nothing to do with each other. Their apparent link could be no more than a coincidence. In this case, though we have questioned whether there is causal relationship between ice cream sales and car accidents, we cannot say that there isn't a link between the two. They are linked by the third piece of evidence that during the summer there are more people going to Bournemouth. If we want to say that there is no more than coincidence to two pieces of evidence, then we need to go beyond the possibility that there is something that links the two. For example:

  fact 1: dolphins are regularly spotted in the sea at Bournemouth;

  fact 2: the magazine *Harpers and Queen* has described Bournemouth as 'the next coolest city on the planet'.

  These two facts might be related but they are probably no more than two unrelated facts that both happen to be about Bournemouth (which isn't in fact a city).

What about the next two?

fact 1: many pop stars and footballers go to Bournemouth;

fact 2: house prices nearby are exceeded only by those in central London, Singapore, and Hong Kong (all very, very expensive places).

Think how you would assess these two facts in terms of a *post hoc* argument.

- Of course, some things are, as we have seen, likely to be related in a simple causal way. The increase in the number of car accidents in the summer in Bournemouth is almost certainly explained by the increase in the number of people in the place compared to the rest of the year. Similarly, the increase in sales of ice cream is explained in a simple way by the increase in people in Bournemouth in the summer.

STRAW MAN

Imagine that you have two figures in front of you. One is a statue made from marble; the other is a scarecrow, made from bits of sack and filled with straw. The statue is a very good representation of a human figure; the scarecrow sags and droops, and has a carrot for a nose. Now with your hand, knock one over. Poor scarecrow.

We find this **straw man** in arguments too.

Look at the following example:

> *There are many good things about modern society. We can travel long distances quickly and in comfort. We have homes that are comfortable, with a variety of things that make our life more pleasant. However, there are some people that see these good things as things we should not welcome. These people call themselves 'Greens' and they oppose cars, the building of roads, air travel, the generation of electricity, and all other things that make our life comfortable. In short, Greens oppose progress. Therefore we shouldn't support them in any way.*

Look at the structure of this argument.

R: People who call themselves 'Greens' see the good things of modern society as things we should not welcome.

IC: Greens oppose progress.

C: Therefore we shouldn't support them in any way.

An evaluation of this argument shows that the intermediate conclusion can be drawn with few problems. If we see the good things of modern society as resulting from 'progress' then it follows straightforwardly. What about the move from IC to C? This requires the assumption that 'we should not support those who oppose progress'. If the author believes this, then the conclusion follows again straightforwardly. So, if this argument is flawed, what is the weakness in it?

The answer is the reason itself. Do people called 'Greens' oppose everything that makes our life comfortable? There might be some people who oppose all aspects of modern society, but to describe all people who call themselves 'Green' in this way is a significant exaggeration. As a result, the argument is weak because part of it is simply not true. What the author has done is to produce an argument against the Greens that is overdrawn in the sense that, given that the reason is not true, so the conclusion cannot be drawn without additional reasoning that is.

A further point is that the author's exaggeration is likely to come from their wish to show the Greens in a bad light. They have set up this version of the Greens' beliefs in order to discredit them. They have set up a *straw man*. As we have seen the term describes something that is easy to knock down. The straw man description of the Greens' beliefs provides the author with an easy way of knocking down support for them. And, like with our statue and scarecrow, the first is an accurate representation, the second is not so.

Look at the same argument with a small adjustment.

R: Some people who call themselves 'Greens' see the good things of modern society as things we should not welcome.

IC:Such Greens oppose progress.

C: Therefore we shouldn't support them in any way.

The introduction of the word 'some' has changed it significantly. The author has no longer set up a straw man by exaggerating the position, in that there are presumably some people who call themselves 'Greens' who do oppose progress because they oppose modern developments. In this new version, with the disappearance of the straw man, so the conclusion no longer looks overdrawn.

We have seen that if we think an author has used a straw man in their argument, they have done all of the following:

• deliberately distorted their opponent's position;

- deliberately distorted their opponent's position in order to present it as a very weak argument;

- deliberately distorted their opponent's position as a very weak argument in order to knock it down (to discredit it).

What they have not done in putting up this straw man is to attack their opponent(s). They have not attacked their character, their honesty, or whatever. They might even have gone out of their way to present their opponents as decent people.

> *People who call themselves 'Greens' are caring, decent people. Unfortunately, they oppose cars, the building of roads, air travel, the generation of electricity, and all other things that make our life comfortable. In short, Greens oppose progress. Therefore we shouldn't support them in any way.*

An author who attacks their opponent is doing something else. We meet this flaw next.

AD HOMINEM

This Latin term means 'against the man' (or person). The full term is *argumentum ad hominem* and this translates as 'argument against the man'. In this type of argument, the author is not misrepresenting their opponent's argument as with the straw man argument. With the **ad hominem** argument, the author is attacking their opponent in some way *rather than* their argument.

> *There are many good things about modern society. We can travel long distances quickly and in comfort. We have homes that are comfortable, with a variety of things that make our life more pleasant. However, there are some people that see these good things as things we should not welcome. Some of these people call themselves 'Greens' and they oppose the way in which cars pollute our towns and cities, the way in which road-building programmes spoils our countryside, and so on. These people are likely to be unemployed, living off the State, and have long straggly beards. Therefore we certainly shouldn't take any notice of people's arguments who are like that.*

It's pretty clear what's going on here. The author's conclusion is drawn on the basis of an attack upon the Greens for their apparent lifestyle and appearance. The conclusion is straightforwardly overdrawn in that, in this argument, the Greens' apparent lifestyle and appearance is irrelevant to whether or not we should 'take any notice' of their argument.

Interestingly, the Greens' argument is not misrepresented, so there is no straw man going on here.

You might think that there's a look of a straw man, in that the attack on the Greens misrepresents them in terms of their lifestyle and appearance. This is true, but a straw man flaw is reserved for the setting up of a distorted argument. The author has this time not misrepresented their opponents' argument, but something about their opponents.

Are negative comments about other people always examples of weak arguments?

> *Many people protested violently near where the leaders of the G8 Summit met in the summer of 2005, hurling missiles and attacking the police. These people don't have to make complex decisions on a wide range of political, economic, and social issues. They don't have to weigh up the interests and needs of different groups. They don't have to face voters in elections. The leaders of the G8 have to do all of these things. These violent protestors can see things in simple terms – stop starvation; cancel debts – because they don't have to make these complex decisions. Cancelling billions of pounds of debts owed to banks and such like isn't a simple thing. These people really should try to see that things are much more complex than they think they are.*

This argument criticises those who protested violently at the 2005 G8 summit on the grounds that they over-simplify the issue of cancelling the debt of developing countries. In this way, the author has questioned their understanding of the issues in order to conclude that they should try to see things differently. The people who protested violently are not criticised as such: only their argument.

TU QUOQUE

Here's another weakness in argument that has a Latin name. *Tu quoque* (pronounced 'tu' like 'tyou' and 'quoque' like 'kwokway') means no more than 'you too' or 'you also'. In this flaw, the author is using reasoning that amounts to saying that something can be justified (though normally wrong) if other people are doing it. The next example shows this.

> *Thousands of drivers each day break the speed limit. Virtually none of them gets caught by speed cameras and traffic patrols. As a result, the few who do are right to complain that they shouldn't be seen as having done anything wrong.*

The argument concludes that people who get caught speeding are 'right to complain that they shouldn't be seen as having done anything wrong'. This conclusion is drawn from no more than the reason that thousands of drivers break the speed limit every day without being caught. Why is this conclusion overdrawn? Obviously, as always, because the reasoning is insufficient for the conclusion. The author concludes that speeding motorists *have done nothing wrong* on the strength of lots of people speeding. This goes much too far, and in some ways borders on the irrelevant.

What happens with a different conclusion?

> *Thousands of drivers each day break the speed limit. Virtually none of them gets caught by speed cameras and traffic patrols. The few who do are therefore very unlucky.*

This argument is doing something very different from the previous one. It is concluding that the people who get caught speeding are unlucky rather than having done no wrong. This conclusion doesn't look overdrawn at all. This is because the reasons are highly relevant to the conclusion. In the earlier version, the reasons were not relevant to a judgement of whether or not speeding is acceptable.

Tu quoque arguments don't have to look like the first one above. They can have the form 'something is wrong only if other things (supposedly like it) are also wrong'.

> *It is often argued that computer games that have a violent theme should be banned. This is because, it is claimed, these games encourage young people to be aggressive and not to care about what happens to other people in the game. But if we look at all sports (from chess to cricket, from fencing to football), then young people playing them are encouraged to be aggressive and to not let worries about the other side losing get in the way of winning. Should Chelsea play gently with West Ham? Given that aggression is a central feature of the playing of sport, we should not ban violent computer games.*

In this argument, the author presents a counter-argument at the beginning (that violent computer games should be banned because they encourage aggression and a lack of care about others). They respond to this by arguing that, since all sports do what violent computer games are supposed to do, (and since – assumption – we are happy to have young people playing sports), then violent computer games shouldn't be banned. You can see the 'you too' element of this argument: violent computer games are OK only because sports are OK. The person who wanted to put the counter-argument could respond by saying that there are still reasons to ban violent computer games. (For example, they are much more aggressive than any sport.)

CIRCULAR ARGUMENTS

> *This train is a no-smoking service. Therefore passengers are not allowed to smoke in any of the carriages, toilets, and vestibules.*

In this short argument, the conclusion is contained in the reason. All the second sentence does is to clarify the significance of the first. It could be that, when the train manager/conductor announces this over a train's public address system, that it what is intended. But, as an argument, it is entirely **circular**: it ends where it started.

SLIPPERY SLOPES

If circular arguments don't really go anywhere (just back to 'Go'), then **slippery slopes** go much too far. If you've been on a toboggan run, you'll know that, as you sit at the top on your toboggan, there is the sense that once you've pushed yourself a little at the top, the next stop is the bottom. And the bottom looks a long way away.

Slippery slope arguments start with one reason, then make big jumps to other reasons, as they hurtle towards their conclusion. Hold tight: there's one coming.

> *The popularity of the Harry Potter books is a worrying thing. They deal with magic, and strange characters that live in a bizarre world. If children read these, they will believe that magic is real, and that such a world is only a train ride away. Believing magic to be real, they will reject science. In rejecting science, they're going to reject very important ways in which we think. (For example, they will stop thinking that the Moon is a satellite of the Earth, and will think of it as an entity that can get involved in our affairs.) With science rejected, medicine will be rejected and replaced with bundles of herbs, books of spells, and cauldrons. Cars will be replaced by horses. Our whole way of life will crumble. We will enter a new Dark Age. To stop this happening, we must stop children reading the Harry Potter books. Now.*

As you can see, that was quite a journey from reading Harry Potter books to a new Dark Age. The problem with the argument was that, quite simply, we took a lot of very big (and highly questionable) steps on the way to the conclusion. If you look at any of them, you will see this.

The Harry Potter books deal with magic.

If children read them, they will believe magic to be real.
If they believe magic to be real, they will reject science.
If they reject science, then medicine will be rejected.

Though the last 'if… then' is acceptable (given that Western medicine is based entirely on science), we have a series of very questionable steps to get to this position.

The response to a slippery slope argument is that the conclusion is very heavily overdrawn because the reasoning, being so dubious, is nothing like sufficient for it.

However, this is not to say that all arguments that work their way through a series of steps are slippery slope arguments.

> *Some caves have been discovered with paintings on the wall that are many thousands of years old. They are certainly older than any others that have been discovered. There is a lot of public interest in these paintings, especially as the images of wild animals in them are so clear and bright. However, we shouldn't let people in the caves to see them. If we did, then their breath will make the caves damp. With dampness, the images will start to deteriorate very quickly. Once this happens, there will be no way to restore them to their present stunning state. We will then lose the opportunity to study how the images were made. This would be a complete tragedy.*

This argument, like the Harry Potter one, went through a series of stages to its conclusion that we shouldn't let people into the caves to look at the paintings. Even the intermediate conclusion isn't too overdrawn, despite its rather dramatic language ('a complete tragedy').

So slippery slopes go too far, too quickly. Watch out for them.

RESTRICTING THE OPTIONS

This is a type of weakness in argument that is often found in some daily newspapers. An issue will be seen as either black or white, good or bad, this policy or its complete opposite.

> *We must either allow people to defend their own homes with whatever means they choose, or we are saying to burglars 'Come in, take what you like, do what you like'. The Government has no choice but to change the law to allow the first of these.*

This argument is a good example of the popular newspaper approach to issues. Either do something clearly good or do something clearly bad: therefore do the first. You will have noticed that there's an element of straw man going on here too, with the way the second alternative is being presented: no government is going to adopt such a policy as encouraging burglars to burgle.

The problem with this type of argument is that its reasons are a distortion of what is the case. For this reason, these arguments are sometimes called 'false dilemmas'. In this example, there are many things that could be done short of either of the two positions. These could include the following examples:

• We could provide Government grants to fit burglar alarms to people's houses.

• We could allow people to defend themselves using only 'reasonable force'.

• We could increase the penalty for burglary to try to deter people from doing this.

This is not to deny that sometimes we are faced with a limited choice. (Should I vote for the proposal, vote against it, or not vote at all?) But normally, the weakness of a restriction of options is precisely that: there are far more options than the author has given.

> *The developed world can either turn its back on the suffering of the developing world, or it can solve the problem of poverty overnight. It's obvious that the developed world should make poverty history.*

Unfortunately, much of the argument about relieving the debt of the developing world tends to be in this restricted option form: we either help by cancelling debt or we don't help at all if we don't cancel debt. Think of the range of choices that could fit in between these two positions.

MAKING IRRELEVANT APPEALS

Arguments, as we have seen, are weak because the reasons do not support the conclusion with sufficient strength. There is a group of such weaknesses that come under the heading of making **irrelevant appeals**.

Appeal to popularity

> *Surveys have shown that between 60–70% of the population of the UK believe that global warming is taking place. When you have a figure as high as that, there must*

be a lot of truth in the claim that global warming is happening.

This argument uses one piece of evidence on the percentage of the UK population who believe that global warming is happening to draw a conclusion about the 'truth' of global warming. What is the problem with this argument?

The problem is that the reason is quite simply insufficient to draw the conclusion. The truth about global warming is not determined by what percentage of the population believes that it is happening. The truth is determined by experts applying their understanding to evidence such as changes in temperatures around the world. Is there a similar problem in the next example?

Ever since capital punishment was abolished in the 1960s, public opinion in this country has been in favour of bringing it back. Given that governments are meant to listen to the people, it should therefore be brought back.

We have a pretty clear **appeal to popularity** in this argument. But, on this occasion, the author of the argument has made it clear why such an appeal is relevant: 'governments are meant to listen to the people'. If this is accepted, then the public support for bringing back the death penalty is relevant to the conclusion that it should be. A different form of this argument follows:

Ever since capital punishment was abolished in the 1960s, public opinion in this country has been in favour of bringing it back. This is because the majority of the population believes that the death penalty acts to deter people from committing murder. Therefore it should be brought back.

In this argument, we have something similar going on to the previous one. But there is a crucial difference. This is that the conclusion is based only on the reason that the majority of the population believes that the death penalty is a deterrent. This time, like with the global warming example, people might be wrong. Their belief could be tested by looking at evidence. For example, we could have a look at what has happened in the US where people are executed.

What we can see then is that appeals to popularity are examples of weakness in argument only when popular belief in something can be questioned.

A survey has shown that 68% of people in the UK prefer taking their holidays abroad. They say, for example, that the weather is better and hotels are cheaper. So UK holiday resorts need to concentrate on ensuring that, though they can't control the weather, they provide a range of facilities that will appeal to holidaymakers.

In this example, the conclusion is drawn on the strength of evidence that 68% of people in the UK see foreign holidays as better than those taken in the UK because of things like the better weather and the lower price of hotels. Here, of course, we could say that these people are wrong to think this. We could argue that a week in Brighton or Torquay can beat anything that Majorca or Nice can offer. We could compare hotel prices (and, much less hopefully, the weather). But in this argument, we can't say that people's preference for foreign holidays is irrelevant to the conclusion. It is straightforwardly relevant, such that the conclusion doesn't look overdrawn.

We have seen then that, in judging the significance of appeals to popularity, we need to look at the central point of relevance. Put simply, is what people believe sufficiently relevant to the conclusion being drawn?

> *76% of married women said that they would not tolerate their husband being unfaithful to them. Men should therefore think very carefully before having an affair if they want to keep their marriage safe.*

In this example, the evidence acts as a sufficiently relevant reason for the conclusion. In the next one, it doesn't.

> *76% of married women said that they would not tolerate their husband being unfaithful to them. Therefore having an affair is unjustified.*

You should be able to see then that, just because an author uses evidence regarding the 'popularity' of something, this does not mean that they have a weak argument. It is only when this evidence is not (sufficiently) relevant to the conclusion, that we can say that the argument is weak because they have appealed (wrongly) to popularity.

Appeal to authority

Arguments will often contain evidence or claims that come from those who are meant to be seen as people (or organisations) with authority. By this we mean that they are seen as having special skills, knowledge, experience, and so on. Very often this is entirely straightforward.

> *A report was issued in 2005 by the Carnegie Endowment for International Peace. It was produced after more than 150 experts from 20 countries looked at the problems*

of preventing the growth of nuclear weapons. The report recommends that decisions need to be taken over the next few years to restrict the supply of the materials that can be used to make nuclear weapons. It is therefore clear that we should look at ways of ensuring that those countries that have nuclear materials (such as the UK and the US) control what happens to them.

In this argument, the conclusion is based on the recommendation of the report produced by 'more than 150 experts from 20 countries'. The authority of such experts is sufficient for us to see that the conclusion is not based on anything that could be called irrelevant. We might, of course, still disagree on the exact conclusion, especially when experts themselves can disagree. But, in this case, there isn't an irrelevant **appeal to authority**.

What does one look like then?

David Baddiel is a well-known comedian. He is seen by some as having considerable talent at what he does. In 2005 he wrote an article for The Times *condemning the decision to have gone to war in Iraq. In that Baddiel is seen as having intelligence and wit, we should pay attention to what he has to say on this subject.*

In this argument, the conclusion that we ought to 'pay attention' to Baddiel's views on the rightness or wrongness of the war in Iraq is based only on people seeing him as having 'intelligence and wit'. This is an irrelevant appeal to Baddiel as an authority, in that whatever judgement we might make about his talent as a comedian, his skills are irrelevant to a judgement on the Iraq war. This is not to say that he might not have useful things to say on the subject, but rather to say that a judgement about the Iraq war should not be based on what he has to say on the subject.

Thus when we are assessing whether or not an appeal to authority is irrelevant, we are looking to see, not whether the 'authority' has expertise, but whether or not this expertise is relevant.

Appeal to pity

Arguments often use information about a person or group of people to draw a conclusion about them. In some cases, this information is used to **appeal to pity**.

Many young people don't go to university because they're not encouraged by their family and school to do so. They can end up working in jobs that don't use all their talents (or have no job at all). They should therefore be given priority over other people when it comes to well-paid, interesting jobs in industries such as banking, insurance, and computing.

In this example, the conclusion is drawn from information given in two reasons.

R1 Many young people don't go to university because they're not encouraged by their family and school to do so.

R2 They can end up working in jobs that don't use all their talents (or have no job at all).

The author takes these reasons as sufficient for the conclusion. To what extent is it overdrawn?

It is considerably overdrawn. The conclusion that we should give priority in giving well-paid, interesting jobs to people who didn't go to university because they weren't encouraged to go relies on no more than an appeal to pity for these people. It isn't as if the author had shown that these people were cleverer, more hard-working, or more creative (or whatever) than those who had gone to university. The information that they are either unemployed or in jobs that don't use all their talents is not enough for us to conclude that they should be given priority. We could make an 'Oh dear' response, and fret that these young people might be miserable. But their unhappiness isn't enough to make us require banks to give them well-paid, interesting jobs rather than the people who've got qualifications (and possibly experience) relevant to the jobs. Oh dear indeed. The appeal to pity has failed to produce a good argument.

Many young people don't go to university because they're not encouraged by their family and school to do so. They can end up working in jobs that don't use all their talents (or have no job at all). We need to make use of everybody's talents. So there should be a scheme set up to help them go to university in order to help them to develop theirs.

In this argument, the author argues very differently. The third reason ('We need to make use of everybody's talents.') adds something very important to this argument. There is no longer an appeal to pity about our frustrated young people who weren't encouraged to go to university. In this argument, the author draws a conclusion which fits well with the reasons. It's a conclusion that is far from being overdrawn.

SPECIAL KINDS OF ARGUMENT CONTENT

We have seen that arguments consist of reasons (often supported by evidence) and conclusions. In this section, we are going to look at particular types of argument content. These are

- analogies

- counter-arguments

- dcfinitions

- principles

- hypothetical arguments

- necessary and sufficient conditions

ANALOGIES

An author might want to give strength to their argument by claiming that something in their argument is like something else. More specifically, they want us to see that if something happens in one situation, then the same thing ought to happen in (what they take to be) another sufficiently similar situation. When an author argues in this way, they are using an **analogy**.

The following argument contains an analogy.

Train services should run on time for most of the time. However, they frequently run late, for a variety of reasons, virtually all of which are preventable. In contrast, TV stations manage day after day to screen programmes that run almost always exactly to time. For example, Coronation Street *comes on, as we're promised, at 7.30 on*

Fridays. We would be rightly appalled if we were told that Coronation Street *was delayed for 22 minutes, and we were faced with nothing but a blank screen. So why is it that rail companies fail day after day to run trains on time? The 7.30 from somewhere to anywhere is frequently delayed. Train companies should try to learn from the experience of TV companies.*

In this example, the author takes the situation of TV companies as sufficiently similar to that of rail companies in order to argue that trains should run in time. When you look at the argument, you can see that the argument consists mostly of the reference to TV schedules.

This *assumption of sufficient similarity* is a necessary feature of the use of an analogy. Thus to see if an analogy is relevant to an author's argument, we have to consider whether the author is right to assume sufficient similarity.

In this example, to what extent is the author's analogy of TV stations sufficiently similar to rail companies?

Similarities

- Both TV stations and rail companies publish details of times.

- Both TV stations and rail companies are large organisations.

- Both TV stations and rail companies provide a service directly to the public.

Differences

- TV stations normally use pre-recorded programmes; rail services are always 'live'.

- There are (probably) fewer things to go wrong with the broadcast of TV programmes than with running a train service (the effect of the weather, the impact of a broken-down train, etc.)

- As a continuation of the previous point, the role of the consumer is very different between the two services. Passengers can themselves cause delays (pulling emergency handles, people walking on the tracks, and so on). TV viewers can have no obvious direct effect on the timing of programmes.

Specific source of weakness

- When TV companies do broadcast live events, things often happen to affect their timetable of programmes. For example, when televised football matches go to extra time, then programmes are rescheduled, often resulting in programmes being cancelled.

So how good is the analogy between rail companies and TV stations? Though our list of similarities and differences had three points in each, the differences have a greater significance. Importantly, the first difference greatly reduces the significance of the first similarity. Though both rail companies and TV stations both use and publish timetables, the issue of 'live' services and pre-recorded services is crucial. The specific source of weakness in the analogy is very significant in that, when TV companies are in the same 'live' position as rail companies, they also reschedule (including cancel) their services.

Looking at the issue of sufficient similarity, we find that the author was wrong to assume this. In consequence, since the analogy is not successful, so the argument is greatly weakened. (It is not entirely disposed of since, as we saw, the author also argues that train companies run late because of 'preventable reasons'.)

A good analogy, then, is one in which the degree of similarity is sufficient for the argument (or at least that part of it) to work.

Look at the next example.

> *A railway company is like an airline. They both move lots of people from various points A to various points B. Eastern Airways almost always run their schedules to time. They have to deal with weather (a factor beyond their control), with equipment that needs frequent maintenance, and with the human factor of passengers, baggage handlers, pilots, and so on, all of whom have the potential to cause disruption by failure to arrive, and so on. If Eastern Airways can fly people to destinations on time, then so too should train companies be able to run their services on time.*

So is a railway company like an airline? In this example, the author explicitly claims that it is. But this time they have gone further. They have explained why it is. Both airlines and railway companies move people around, and both are subject to the weather, how well equipment works, and 'the human factor'. In that their conclusion is based entirely on this analogy, it is crucial for the argument that the analogy is as good as the author claims. We approach an evaluation of this claimed analogy in the same way as before.

Similarities

- The author has already given us two very important similarities.

- Both railway companies and airlines are dependent on other sections/systems/ organisations to operate on time (for example, what's going on at other stations/ airports).

Differences

- The fact that trains run on tracks and aeroplanes have no such limitation in terms of being able to move from A to B is significant. Tracks need maintenance, but the sky doesn't.

- Railways have a much more complicated system to operate. The signalling system, for example, is not equivalent in its extent and complexity to air traffic control (that largely operates only at the airport, whereas signalling operates throughout the rail network).

Specific sources of weakness

- Airlines do reschedule flights (including cancellation).

- Flights can be delayed by factors such as the weather.

Given these sources of weakness, the author's argument suffers attack from an unexpected direction. In that airlines are indeed like train companies, we can expect trains to be delayed for the same sorts of reasons that planes are.

In this example, the author has overstated the analogy. Though the similarity between airlines and railway companies is greater than that between TV stations and rail companies, there are still important differences. Furthermore, as we saw, the sources of weakness are a problem for the author's argument. In that the argument used no more than the analogy, the conclusion is overdrawn.

There is, of course, another source of evaluation of this argument. This is that the author uses only Eastern Airways as the evidence to support the analogy. It could be that this airline is unusual in being so good.

We have referred to the assumption of sufficient similarity as a necessary feature of the use of analogies. But using them involves something else as well. This is the *appeal to the value of consistency*. By this we mean that, in using an analogy, the author is stressing that we should be consistent in the way in which we argue. In our previous example, the author is in effect saying that, given that Eastern Airways is sufficiently similar to rail companies, then we are inconsistent if we think that we should judge the two differently.

You will remember when we looked at assumptions that we found the negative test useful. It was explained there that the reason this test worked was because there would be something very odd about someone believing something and at the same time believing its opposite. To a large extent, this is going on with the appeal to the value of consistency. The test of its relevance is, of course, to go back to the assumption of sufficient similarity. If the two situations are not sufficiently similar, then there is no problem with consistency. If they are, then the author is making a relevant appeal.

In all of the following arguments, the author uses an analogy. Evaluate the relevance of each analogy, using the framework that we have used above.

(1) Restricting the hours that pubs and clubs can open in order to stop people binge-drinking is like banning the sale of petrol on certain times during the week to stop people using their car so much. It's obvious, then, that we should not restrict the hours in which alcohol can be sold.

(2) Research into space is like research into who was Jack the Ripper. Interesting and intriguing certainly, but in the end something that makes no difference to the way in which we live our lives. Therefore we should spend our money on things of much greater value than space research.

(3) It's sometimes said that people shouldn't go on foreign holidays because, in doing so, they reduce employment in the British holiday trade. But this is like saying we shouldn't buy foreign goods because this also reduces employment in Britain. In that we're very happy buying foreign goods, from toys to cars, we should not listen to those who argue that our holidays should be spent in this country.

COUNTER-ARGUMENTS

It is quite common to find that authors include something of their opponent's position within the argument they're presenting. They do this normally in order to knock it down. It's no more than saying 'Some people believe this, but I'm going to show you why they shouldn't'. So, when an author presents the opposing point of view, you should not see this as them being contradictory. Look at the next example.

Having big music events featuring many famous artists is seen as a way of solving problems such as poverty and injustice. By focusing people's attention on these problems, it is argued, action will be taken to address them, so we should encourage people to organise such events. However, there is little evidence that these events have any lasting effect. They give the appearance of action, without the reality. People can sing their hearts out and yell slogans for the crowd to repeat, but in the end poverty and injustice are the product of a complex of all sorts of factors: economic, historical, political, geographical, even religious. Feeding the world is therefore much more complicated than singing the words. These events over-simplify the issues and thus should be seen as nothing more than an opportunity for publicity-hungry artists to perform in front of thousands of people. As a result, we should not encourage people to organise such events.

In this argument, the author starts by setting up an argument. The first two sentences are this argument, and end with the conclusion 'so we should encourage people to organise such events'. But as you read on, you realise that the author disagrees with this argument, such that the conclusion of the whole argument is exactly the opposite of this one. What the author has done is to present what we call a **counter-argument** in order to show why it's not a good one. The argument against their own (or counter to their own) has been put there as a target to be shot down. Whether or not it has been effectively dealt with is a different matter.

When you see this type of argument, you will often find that words such as 'however', 'but', and 'on the other hand' indicate what's going on. They indicate that the author's own argument is about to start.

In the above example, there was a counter-argument in the sense that the opposing position was given as a completed argument, with a conclusion. You will also find counter-positions being given which are not completed arguments. We call these counter-claims or counter-assertions. In the next example, the author has presented the opposing position in a form that isn't an argument.

Having big music events featuring many famous artists is seen as a way of solving problems such as poverty and injustice. But there is little evidence that these events have any lasting effect. They give the appearance of action, without the reality. People can sing their hearts out and yell slogans for the crowd to repeat, but in the end poverty and injustice are the product of a complex of all sorts of factors: economic, historical, political, geographical, even religious. Feeding the world is therefore much more complicated than singing the words. These events over-simplify the issues and thus should be seen as nothing more than an opportunity for publicity-hungry artists to perform in front of thousands of people. As a result, we should not encourage people to organise such events.

In this version, the author responds to a claim or assertion that is made, and in exactly the same way as before, responds to it. What is happening in terms of the structure of the argument hasn't changed. As explained above, the word 'but' indicates the beginning of the author's own argument.

Counter-arguments or counter-claims don't have to appear at the beginning of an argument, although they often do because of what the author is doing (setting up a position in order to knock it down). If you were to structure an argument which contained one, then you would include it as part of that structure.

If you are asked to produce an argument that contains a counter-argument or counter-claim, then all you need to do is to present something from the other point of view. You would then respond to it, by showing why this opposing position had a problem.

Counter-arguments or counter-claims/assertions present a version of the opposing position. It is important that you distinguish these from what we can call 'scene-setting'. Sometimes an author presents some information that is relevant to the argument, but which is not part of a counter-position. They are giving information in order to provide a context for the argument.

> *In Poland, dogs (or, more specifically, puppies) are sold in open-air markets similar to car boot sales. On a Sunday morning, you can go to one of these markets and come away with anything from a St Bernard to a Yorkshire Terrier. In the UK we don't sell dogs like this. If people want a puppy, then they have to go to the home of the breeder. But perhaps it doesn't matter how puppies are bought. The important thing is how dogs are looked after. Dogs are very intelligent animals. Their capacity to learn tricks is well-known, but what is less well-known is their ability to understand language. Some dogs have been found to have an understanding of words that matches that of young children. Dogs have other very good qualities. They are loyal to their owners. They are forgiving. They are very affectionate. It is clear then that dogs should be treated with considerable respect for their intelligence and for all their other qualities.*

In this passage, the author provides an argument that concludes that 'dogs should be treated with considerable respect for their intelligence and for all their other qualities'. But the first part of the passage isn't part of the argument as such. The information about how puppies are sold in Poland sets the scene for the author to develop an argument about dogs, but it doesn't form part of the reasoning. If you read the passage again, starting in the middle with the sentence 'Dogs are very intelligent animals', then you can see that the author's argument begins here.

What you have seen in the previous passage is that the information about Poland was not being used to describe a counter-position. We don't know from the passage whether or not the author thinks that puppies being sold in markets is worse than buying from the breeder's home. Even if they did think this, they make the statement 'perhaps it doesn't matter how puppies are bought'. So, whether or not the author agrees with the method, the author has not presented the information as a counter-argument or counter-claim.

DEFINITIONS

We sometimes find that an argument contains a **definition**. What exactly is a definition? It is a statement of what exactly something is. (You might have spotted that this is a definition of a definition.) An author might want to use a definition as part of their argument or they might want to argue such that they conclude with a definition.

In arguments where a definition is used as part of an argument, an author might simply state what something means. This stated definition could then be used as a reason in the argument. The next example does this.

> *There are parts of most cities and towns that are described as unsafe. Some ways of driving a car are also seen as unsafe. Lots of other activities (such as bungee jumping) are also described in this way. So all of these places and activities must have something in common. Should 'safe' be seen as a state in which there are no risks at all? No, because no situation or activity could ever be like that. (Even being in bed could have risks of injury from falling out of it, or the ceiling falling down, and so on.) A much better way of defining 'safe' is to say that something is safe if the risk attached to it of something unwelcome happening is acceptably low. In this way, being in bed is obviously safe because of the very low risks involved. Safe driving is going on when the risk of accidents is acceptably low. Given that, when we're talking about safety, we're still talking about some level of risk, we should not criticise the Government if unwelcome things still happen in our daily lives.*

In this argument the author provides a definition of the word 'safe' in order to draw a conclusion about the Government. The definition is 'something is safe if the risk attached to it of something unwelcome happening is acceptably low'. They consider a counter-definition first ('a state in which there are no risks at all') and argue against this by giving a reason ('because no situation or activity could ever be like that'). As you can see, the argument is centrally concerned with defining 'safe' such that the definition provides the reason for the conclusion. In this example, an evaluation of the argument is very much concerned with an evaluation of the definition used.

In the next example, the author draws a conclusion after having tried and then (deliberately) failed to define something.

> *These days we are constantly being urged to be fit. TV programmes such as 'Fit Club' shame people who are not able to run around a track or do press-ups. Gyms try to get our business by portraying images of supposedly attractive people in tight clothing smilingly running on a running machine. But what do we mean by 'fitness'? Is it the ability to run for half an hour on a running machine? Is it the ability to walk ten miles? Is it the ability to play certain sports such as badminton or squash without becoming unduly tired? Is fitness something that changes with age, such that a fit seventeen year-old is different from a fit seventy year-old? Given that it might be all or none of these things, the problem of defining fitness means that we have no idea what we're pursuing. Paying money to pursue something that can't be defined seems a waste of money. Thus cancel your gym subscription and spend it on something that is clearly good for you, like a holiday.*

In this argument, the author uses the problem of trying to define something in order to draw their conclusion. They give three definitions of 'fitness' and then an issue with defining it (age). They then suggest that all or none of these could be relevant in order to argue that 'we have no idea of what we're pursuing' when we pursue fitness. The author goes even further in the next sentence by claiming that fitness 'can't be defined'. What is the weakness in the author's argument?

This is the problem we identified in the section on 'Evaluating Arguments'. The author has restricted the options. Having given us some definitions and one problem with definition, the author argues that fitness can't be defined. But, of course, there could still be a definition of fitness that the author hasn't considered, but which would be acceptable by most people. (In fact, one definition of fitness includes nine components including strength, power, agility, flexibility, and co-ordination. In this way, we can see that the author was correct in arguing that fitness could be a number of different things, but incorrect in concluding that therefore it couldn't be defined.) Because of the restriction of the options problem, the conclusion is overdrawn. Look out for this in arguments. An author can tilt their argument in a particular direction by using (or, at least, claiming) problems of definition.

In some arguments the definition of something significant in the argument is often assumed rather than stated. This can be a problem if the definition has a considerable bearing on the argument. This problem occurs in the next argument.

In Europe the environment causes 100,000 deaths of children each year. This is completely unacceptable. The governments of Europe need to get together to find ways of reducing this annual slaughter of the innocents.

The crucial definition required in order to be able to assess this argument is that of the word 'environment'. Does it mean 'pollution' and only 'pollution'? Does it mean 'quality of water, sanitation facilities, air quality'? Or what? In fact, the term as it is used in this argument includes the safety of the roads. Furthermore the figure of 100,000 includes not just deaths on the roads, but also drownings, poisonings, and other accidents. In this way, the definition of the term 'environment' is being used in a much broader sense than we would normally use it. The assumed definition needed to be made explicit for there to be a proper evaluation of the argument.

PRINCIPLES

Principles are general statements of how things ought to be. Examples are the following:

Rich countries should always help poor ones.

All students applying to university should be chosen on the basis of their A-level performance rather than which school they come from.

People are entitled to choose the sex of their baby.

Principles can be used by an author as one of the reasons supporting a conclusion, as the only reason, or as the conclusion itself. They could be assumed in an argument. They could even appear as part of a counter-position that the author responds to.

Animals should not suffer any avoidable pain. Therefore they shouldn't ever be used in experiments where pain would be involved, whatever might be gained from such experiments. As a result, we must look at alternative ways of testing drugs.

This argument is a very simple one. It uses the principle in the first sentence to draw the conclusion in the second (which becomes an intermediate conclusion for the main conclusion in the third sentence).

You will see from this example that a principle is very demanding when it is used as a reason. In that a principle is a general statement, an author can't use it at the same time as a particular exception. The next example should clarify this point.

Animals should not suffer any avoidable pain. Therefore, except when there's a clear medical benefit, they shouldn't ever be used in experiments if they suffer pain. As a result, where there's no clear medical benefit from animal experiments, we must look at alternative ways of testing drugs.

In this second version, the author contradicts their own principle. If animals shouldn't suffer any avoidable pain, then the exception the author gives (indeed any exception to it) rejects this principle. This shows that principles are very powerful reasons. They are powerful in the sense that, as long as the author doesn't have the problem of including an exception as in the above example, they permit a strong conclusion to be drawn from them. They are also powerful in the sense that the author might need no further reasoning.

In the next example, additional reasoning is used.

Animals should not suffer any avoidable pain. Lots of drugs which have been tested on animals have been shown to be safe with animals but have gone on to be dangerous for humans. For example, a drug for arthritis showed as safe with animals but has killed up to 60,000 people. Therefore animals shouldn't ever be used in medical experiments in which pain is involved, whatever might be gained from such experiments. As a result, we must look at alternative ways of testing drugs.

In this example, the intermediate conclusion is drawn from two reasons.

R1: Animals should not suffer any avoidable pain.

R2: Lots of drugs which have been tested on animals have been shown to be safe with animals but have gone on to be dangerous for humans.

IC: Therefore animals shouldn't ever be used in medical experiments in which pain is involved, whatever might be gained from such experiments.

C: As a result, we must look at alternative ways of testing drugs.

As you can see, though the argument is stronger in the sense that there are now two independent reasons being offered, the first (R1) was enough for the conclusion to be drawn. In fact, the principle in R1 would still have been enough even if the author had come up with all sorts of success stories for animal testing of drugs.

119

In looking for principles, you need to look for general statements like 'animals should not suffer any avoidable pain'. They are not the same as what we can call slogans. 'Make poverty history' is a call to action, a slogan that is used to encourage action. But it is not in itself a principle. 'Poverty can never be justified. Therefore get rid of poverty as soon as possible' is an argument using a principle. The slogan 'Make poverty history' doesn't explain why we should. For example, it could be that poverty reflects a poor use of the world's natural resources.

You will have seen that principles are very demanding. This is both their strength and their weakness. Their strength comes from allowing a strong conclusion to be drawn. Their weakness comes from the problem that they can't tolerate any exceptions. The next example illustrates this problem.

> *On the London Underground, there are 6,000 CCTV cameras. The French have fewer than a thousand on their equivalent in Paris, the Metro. Though, in a democratic country, privacy cannot be sacrificed for security, the French are right to be very interested in London's efforts to reduce the risk of terrorism. Therefore we should take comfort from the fact that the Underground is probably safer than the Metro.*

In this argument, the author's principle that 'in a democratic country, privacy cannot be sacrificed for security' rules out any support for the use of CCTV cameras.

ACTIVITY 9

Which of the following is a principle?
(A) Liberty must be sacrificed for the sake of security against terrorism.
(B) Standards of education must rise much faster over the next ten years.
(C) Wage increases must not be allowed to increase more than the country can afford.

HYPOTHETICAL ARGUMENTS

Both reasons and conclusions (and thus complete arguments) can be given in a hypothetical form. By this we mean that they can have the form of 'if this is the case, then that is the case. If that is the case, then we should do something'. Look at the next example.

In the US there have been attempts by people who have become obese to sue fast food companies. They argue that their obesity has been caused by eating the food, such as burgers, sold by these companies. However, if these people were aware of the risks of obesity from eating such fast food, then they have no case against the companies. (It would be like people suing holiday companies for becoming ill as a result of sitting out in the sun for too long.) They must have known the risks, therefore they have no case.

This argument uses the **hypothetical** reason 'if these people were aware of the risks of obesity from eating such fast food, then they have no case against the companies'. In the final sentence, the author moves away from the hypothetical position to one that is no longer hypothetical – 'they must have known the risks' – and so draws a conclusion that is also not hypothetical. (You might have spotted the analogy with holiday companies in the argument. For good practice, have a go at doing an assessment of this analogy.)

What would this argument look like with a hypothetical conclusion? Like this:

In the US there have been attempts by people who have become obese to sue fast food companies. They argue that their obesity has been caused by eating the food, such as burgers, sold by these companies. However, if these people were aware of the risks of obesity from eating such fast food, then they have no case against the companies. If they have no case against the companies, then fast food can continue to be sold without any restrictions.

The last sentence of this argument is a hypothetical conclusion. It is not the same as saying 'fast food can continue to be sold without any restrictions'. By the time we get to the conclusion, the author hasn't established whether or not people were aware of the risks of obesity from eating fast food.

In the next example, another layer of hypothetical reasoning is added.

In the US there have been attempts by people who have become obese to sue fast food companies. They argue that their obesity has been caused by eating the food, such as burgers, sold by these companies. However, if these people were aware of the risks of obesity from eating such fast food, then they have no case against the companies. If, on the other hand, they were not aware of the possibility of such food being addictive, then the companies have a case to answer. It is unlikely that they were aware of this possibility, so they should sue the fast food companies.

In this example, the conclusion is drawn from the second hypothetical reason (regarding addiction). You will notice that the conclusion itself is not a hypothetical one. This is because the author, so to speak, answers the hypothetical reason regarding addiction with the claim that it was, in fact, likely to be the case. The next version doesn't do this, so has a problem.

> *In the US there have been attempts by people who have become obese to sue fast food companies. They argue that their obesity has been caused by eating the food, such as burgers, sold by these companies. However, if these people were aware of the risks of obesity from eating such fast food, then they have no case against the companies. If, on the other hand, they were not aware of the possibility of such food being addictive, then the companies have a case to answer. So these people should sue the fast food companies.*

The problem is, of course, that the author moves from a hypothetical reason to a conclusion that isn't. You can't move straight from saying 'if x is the case, then we should do y', to saying 'therefore we should do y'. You can draw this conclusion *only* if you have shown that x is the case. Thus the conclusion in the above argument is completely overdrawn.

However, you could argue the other way round, from a reason that isn't hypothetical to a conclusion that is.

> *In the US there have been attempts by people who have become obese to sue fast food companies. They argue that their obesity has been caused by eating the food, such as burgers, sold by these companies. Though these people must have been aware of the risks of obesity from eating such fast food, they can't have been aware of the possibility of such food being addictive. So, if these people want to get compensation for the health problems caused by being addicted to fast food, they should sue the fast food companies.*

In this version, the conclusion is a hypothetical one ('if these people…'), but none of the reasoning is. It is a perfectly acceptable way of arguing, and this conclusion cannot be said to be overdrawn.

What do you make of the following argument?

> *If you want to understand pop music, you need to understand Britney Spears. If you want to understand Britney Spears, then you need to understand the town of Kentwood where she was brought up. Therefore, if you understand Kentwood, you'll understand pop music.*

This argument consists of a series of hypothetical statements. It builds itself up in stages, each of which connects with the others. It's a perfectly good argument in the sense that if we accept the hypothetical claims in the first two sentences, then we can accept the hypothetical conclusion in the third. However, the next brief section raises a problem.

NECESSARY AND SUFFICIENT CONDITIONS

In order to see the conclusion of the previous argument about Britney Spears as one that we have to accept, then we have to take the other parts of the argument as having a particular meaning. For example, we have to take 'if you want to understand pop music, you need to understand Britney Spears' to mean 'it is sufficient to understand Britney Spears in order to understand pop music'. Similarly, then, we would have to take 'if you want to understand Britney Spears, then you need to understand Kentwood' to mean that understanding Kentwood is enough in order to understand Britney Spears.

But these statements could be seen differently. Perhaps they are not meant as strongly as we have just seen them. If this is the case, then the conclusion is going to look overdrawn. The first statement 'if you want to understand pop music, you need to understand Britney Spears' could mean 'if you want to understand pop music, it is necessary to understand Britney Spears'. More specifically, it could mean that 'it is necessary but not enough to understand Britney Spears'. In this version, the author is saying that you can't understand pop music unless you understand Britney, but you'll have to understand other people as well in order to have a full understanding. In the same way, the other part of the argument could be seen as 'if you want to understand Britney Spears, then you will need to understand Kentwood, but you'll need to understand other things about her as well'.

What we have here is the business of **necessary and sufficient conditions**. Put simply, we can have any of the following:

- x is a necessary but not a sufficient condition of y;
- x is both a necessary and a sufficient condition of y;
- x is a sufficient but not a necessary condition of y.

An example of the first is 'to become President of the United States, someone must be a US citizen.' Thus, unless you are a US citizen, you can't become President, but being a US citizen is not enough to make you President.

An example of the second is 'to win at least a share in the jackpot in the National Lottery, you need a valid ticket with all six numbers drawn'. Thus, having a valid ticket with all six numbers drawn shown on it is a necessary condition of winning at least a share in the jackpot (you can't win without it, as we frustratingly realise every Saturday). But it is also a sufficient condition, in that (apart, admittedly, from claiming your prize), the ticket is enough.

An example of the third is 'if you are the oldest son of the monarch in the UK, then you are heir to the throne'. Thus, being the eldest son of the monarch is enough to make you heir to the throne. It's a sufficient condition, but it's not necessary. If the monarch has no sons, then the eldest daughter is the heir. If the monarch has no children, then their eldest brother is the heir, and so on.

Of course x might be neither a necessary nor a sufficient condition of y. Reading this book might be neither a necessary nor a sufficient condition of passing AS Critical Thinking, but we hope that it is one or both of them.

ACTIVITY 8: COMMENTARY

(1) *Restricting the hours that pubs and clubs can open in order to stop people binge-drinking is like banning the sale of petrol on certain times during the week to stop people using their car so much. It's obvious, then, that we should not restrict the hours in which alcohol can be sold.*

This argument uses an analogy between buying alcohol and buying petrol as the reason for its conclusion. It needs to be noted that the author intends us to see that restricting the sale of petrol to stop people using their car is something that would be unacceptable. In that the author hasn't stated this, we can see that they must have assumed it. It is this assumed unacceptability that the author uses to argue against restricting the sale of alcohol to prevent binge-drinking. The strength or weakness of the argument depends therefore on the relevance of the analogy.

Similarities

- In both cases, there could be advantages in restricting sales. (The consumption of alcohol can lead to all sorts of problems, including effects on health; motoring can also lead to problems, including pollution and accidents.)

- In both cases, restricting sales through limiting opening-hours could have the effect of reducing consumption.

- In both cases, the product can be bought at times when it is not to be consumed. Thus people can buy alcohol to drink later, and people can fill up their tanks in readiness for a journey.

Differences

- There are very good reasons why people need petrol throughout the day. The obvious one is that, unless they can find petrol available, they are likely to be stranded. There are fewer obviously good reasons why people need to engage in binge-drinking.

- There is nothing illegal about consuming a lot of petrol over a few hours: consuming a lot of alcohol over a short space of time could result in the offence of being 'drunk and disorderly'.

Specific source of weakness

- The parallel of binge-drinking and using petrol for motoring doesn't work, because there is no obvious equivalent of binge-driving. (Driving a lot of miles in a relatively short space of time doesn't necessarily indicate a problem, in that there could be all sorts of legitimate reasons why people do this, such as going on holiday, long-distance lorry driving, and so on.)

In that the author says that the two situations are alike, an assessment of the analogy needs to show whether they are alike or not. Though we have found similarities, the differences and the specific source of weakness are very significant. The point that there is no obvious equivalent of binge-drinking when we think about motoring is a very important one. This is because the two situations are not really the same. Restricting the hours that pubs and clubs can serve alcohol *in order* to stop people binge-drinking is not the same as restricting the sale of petrol in order to stop people using their cars so much. This was a crucial problem with the author's argument.

(2) *Research into space is like research into who was Jack the Ripper. Interesting and intriguing certainly, but in the end something that makes no difference to the way in which we live our lives. Therefore we should spend our money on things of much greater value than space research.*

Similarities

- In both cases, there are questions to which we don't at present have final answers.

- In both cases, it might be said that most people's lives are, as the author says, not really affected by the research.

Differences

- Space research can provide answers to many questions; finding out who was Jack the Ripper provides answers to only one.

- Space research can help us by increasing our knowledge about how the Earth is affected by things such as what's happening in space, such as activity on the Sun (which could affect our climate, amongst other things), the chances of the Earth being hit by an asteroid (and how to deal with this), and so on.

- Space research could lead to us finding new resources to replace ones that might one day be in short supply on Earth.

- The technology of space rockets could be used to improve aircraft design.

- Finding out who was Jack the Ripper cannot be said to have the same number of benefits as space research, some of which have been detailed above.

- People's lives are likely to be much more affected by the outcome of space research than by that of investigating who was Jack the Ripper.

- There are many subjects that benefit from space research: astronomy, obviously, but also physics, chemistry, geology, biology, and so on.

Specific point of weakness

- It could be said that, in each case, there would be benefits in finding answers to questions. For example, in the case of finding out who was Jack the Ripper, there could be benefits in telling us more about serial killers, about detection methods, and so on. In the case of space research, there could be, as above, many benefits. In this way, the author is minimising the benefits of each.

You will see that the analogy is a weak one. There are so many differences between the two situations that the similarities are quite simply swamped. Interestingly, the specific source of weakness finds a similarity between the two, such that the author's argument is again seen as a problem. Because the analogy is so weak, and the author uses no other reasoning, the conclusion is very overdrawn.

(3) *It's sometimes said that people shouldn't go on foreign holidays because, in doing so, they reduce employment in the British holiday trade. But this is like saying we shouldn't buy foreign goods because this also reduces employment in Britain. In that we're very happy buying foreign goods, from toys to cars, we should not listen to those who argue that our holidays should be spent in this country.*

Similarities

* The author provides a similarity to show the relevance of their analogy. This is that of employment.

* Both situations are likely to involve some choice that consumers can make.

Differences

* People will presumably always have a choice between a holiday abroad and one in this country. However, they might not always have a choice between a foreign product and one that is made in this country. An obvious example would be goods such as cars (almost entirely made by foreign companies) and electronic and electrical items.

* People will normally make only one purchase of a foreign holiday each year, whereas they will in the course of a year purchase a wide range and a large quantity of other things, some of which will help British employment and some of which won't.

* Taking a holiday abroad means spending most of the cost abroad; buying a foreign product in this country will still help employment in this country (think about the staff in the shops that sell the foreign goods, for example).

Specific point of weakness

* As suggested in the section on differences, there is a problem with the use of the word 'foreign' in the argument. The author refers to 'foreign' holidays and goods as if the category of 'foreign' is straightforward in each case. Foreign holidays are likely to involve some contribution to British employment (travel agents, airlines, banks providing foreign currency to travellers, and so on.) Foreign goods sold in this country will involve people being employed marketing, distributing, and selling them. In addition, some foreign cars are made in this country. The potential weakness is, then, the extent to which the two things are the same in terms of the separation between 'foreign' and British in each case. If a foreign holiday means that a high percentage of what's spent contributes only to foreign employment, whereas buying a foreign product in this country doesn't, then the two situations are importantly different.

Though the author uses the analogy as a very important part of their argument, there is more than this in the argument. There is also the claim that 'we're very happy buying foreign goods'. Given this reason in the argument, even if the analogy is seen as not very successful, the conclusion can still be drawn. You can see that the author doesn't actually directly address the point about employment. If the analogy is a good one, then, in this case, unusually the author's argument is weakened. This is because they set up the analogy as one that is not meant to persuade us. They presented it as one that didn't work.

What we need to consider then is whether the analogy is as weak as the author wants it to be. You will notice that the author seems to have made it deliberately weak. The reference to reducing 'employment in the British holiday trade' is seen as equivalent to that of reducing employment by not buying foreign goods. But the first is a very specific reference. Perhaps there are particular features of the holiday trade which make it different from say buying things like computers and cars (the after-sales service is an obvious example). Thus the author might be seen as having set up something of a straw man within the analogy.

This last example shows us that sometimes author's use analogies that they themselves think are weak. In these cases, the analogy is something of a counter-argument that the author sets up in order to knock down.

ACTIVITY 9: COMMENTARY

(A) is a principle. It gives a general statement of what should be done. It would provide a strong reason for an argument which, for example, concluded that suspected terrorists should be able to be imprisoned without trial.

(B) is not a principle. It is either a prediction or an instruction, rather than a general statement of what we should do or what should happen. It would not be enough to justify a conclusion like 'therefore we must ensure that education is given priority in spending over all other services'.

(C) is a principle. This provides a general statement of what should (or should not) happen. It could be used to support a conclusion like 'therefore we must resist the threat of strike action from people who want unacceptably high wage increases'.

7

PRODUCING ARGUMENTS

Critical Thinking, as we have seen, is the study of arguments. We have spent our time so far looking at arguments that have already been written. We have learned how to evaluate them for any weaknesses and strengths that they might have.

At some point, however, your skills in working with other people's arguments need to be applied to producing your own. When you are asked to produce an argument, it is clear that you need to write something which has at least one reason and which has a conclusion. If you have no further guidance, then this minimum could be enough. However, in the examination, you are likely to be asked to produce arguments that contain more than this minimum. This could mean two reasons rather than one, and even an intermediate conclusion. But, whatever you need to produce, remember that an argument is completed, so to speak, by a conclusion.

In the examination, the conclusion is in a way given to you. This is because you are being asked to produce arguments in response to one that's already been presented. So, if you know what the conclusion of this argument is, your argument is going to end up concluding either the same thing or its opposite.

To see how this works in practice, we'll work with a passage. So, read the following argument, and try to work out its structure. In particular, find the conclusion.

The death rate among young drivers is significantly higher than that for any other group. More specifically, the death rate among 17–20 year-olds is very much higher than any group (including the next highest, the 21–29 year-olds). When we look at 17–20 year-old males, then we have the highest group of all, more than twice the rate of 17–20 year old females. Even with charging young people more for their insurance, it must still be the case that older (and thus safer) drivers have to subsidise the young ones by their own insurance costs. Young people should be made to have speed-detecting devices fitted to their vehicles. Fitted to a car, these devices are linked to a satellite. The satellite checks the local speed limit and the speed the driver is doing. Insurance companies would be given this information. These devices would be a very effective way of deterring young people from speeding.

There's quite a lot going on in this passage. Apart from the reasons and conclusion(s), there's evidence and an explanation of how speed-detecting devices work. In the end, though, what does the author want to persuade us of? The structure should reveal this.

R1: The death rate among young drivers is significantly higher than that for any other group.

R2: Even with charging young people more for their insurance, it must still be the case that older (and thus safer) drivers have to subsidise the young ones by their own insurance costs.

R3: Insurance companies would have information on drivers' speeding by using speed-detecting devices fitted to cars.

IC: These devices would be a very effective way of deterring young people from speeding.

C: Young people should be made to have speed-detecting devices fitted to their vehicles.

As we considered above, our arguments have to address the author's conclusion. It is not what looks like the general theme of the argument, or a particular point that the author makes on the way to drawing their own conclusion. In addition, it is not our task here to question the evidence that the author uses. We are simply being asked to produce an argument or arguments in response to the author's conclusion. Given this argument, what we are responding to is the author's recommendation that 'Young people should be made to have speed-detecting devices fitted to their vehicles'.

PRODUCING A REASON AGAINST THE AUTHOR'S CONCLUSION

We can build up the argument in stages. We'll start with one reason and produce an argument against the author's conclusion.

Fitting speed-detecting devices to vehicles will be expensive, a cost that will be passed on to all motorists.

Therefore young people should not be made to have speed-detecting devices fitted to their vehicles.

This is a completed argument. It is also a further argument, in the sense that it deals with something that the author hasn't considered. It opens up a new line of reasoning.

PROVIDING EVIDENCE IN SUPPORT OF REASONS

If we are asked to produce evidence in support of our reason(s), or to illustrate the reason(s) in some way, then we need to consider what sort of evidence or illustration would be relevant here. A familiar question here is 'What if I don't know any evidence?'. This is a very good question. You don't know what subjects for the arguments will appear, so there is little or no point in learning lots of evidence just in case they're relevant. There are two simple solutions to this problem.

* You can use hypothetical evidence or illustrations.

* The evidence or illustrations can be 'everyday' information.

HYPOTHETICAL EVIDENCE

Hypothetical evidence or illustration has the advantage that we don't have to know if it's true. We are presenting it as 'if x is the case, then y might happen'. X might not be the case, but it could be very interesting to consider what might happen if it were to be. This is not to say that you can invent the world beyond what's likely, but that you can present possible evidence without knowing if it's correct. Thus, in our example above, hypothetical evidence could work in the following way.

Fitting speed-detecting devices to vehicles will be expensive, a cost that will be passed on to all motorists. If the cost is really high, then some motorists could decide not to insure their vehicles.

Therefore young people should not be made to have speed-detecting devices fitted to their vehicles.

As you can see, the evidence is presented as a possibility and no more than that. We don't know if the cost would be 'really high' or, if it was, whether 'some motorists could decide not to insure their vehicles'. But the evidence doesn't seem unreasonable. It would become unreasonable if the evidence had been 'if the cost is really high, then all motorists would decide not to insure their vehicles'. Though it's still no more than a hypothetical ('if... then'), it's a very unlikely possibility. As a result, its value as evidence is too limited.

EVERYDAY EVIDENCE

You can also use what we can call **everyday evidence** or illustration. By this we mean the sort of information that you're likely to have anyway, the sort that you might get by reading newspapers, listening to the radio, or watching television. A simple example follows.

> *Fitting speed-detecting devices to vehicles will be expensive, a cost that will be passed on to all motorists. Satellite-navigation devices in cars are expensive and these must be similar to the speed-detecting devices.*

This evidence is no more than we could know from what people tell us, knowing that only the more expensive cars have 'sat nav' fitted, from reading an advert for Halfords, or whatever. But the evidence has the effect of supporting the reason that we have used.

In that you're doing Critical Thinking, you wouldn't want to use very limited evidence. For example, if someone said 'my eighteen year-old brother/sister drives a car and he/she doesn't speed', then, of course, we're a bit too everyday with that sort of thing. But then you know that anyway.

PRODUCING A REASON FOR THE AUTHOR'S CONCLUSION

So far, then, we have produced an argument in response to the original one that has one reason supported by evidence leading to a conclusion that is against that of the author. In that further arguments can be either for or against an author's conclusion, we can now look at producing a reason that will support the conclusion that young people should have speed-detecting devices fitted to their vehicles. We are, of course, looking for a reason that the author hasn't used. (Incidentally, as a general rule, you will probably find it easier to come up with reasons against the author, because they're likely to have used up many of the reasons for their position.)

> *The costs to the National Health Service of young people having so many car*
> *accidents are too high. Therefore young people should be made to have speed-*
> *detecting devices fitted to their vehicles.*

Though the original passage used evidence on the relatively high death rate of young drivers, the reason that we have used goes beyond this to look at the wider costs of young people having car accidents. It approaches the author's conclusion from a direction that they hadn't considered at all.

As before, we can add some hypothetical evidence and some everyday evidence.

> *The costs to the National Health Service of young people having so many car*
> *accidents are too high. If the NHS didn't have to treat so many young people*
> *injured in road accidents, then more lives could be saved of people with cancer or*
> *heart disease. Therefore young people should be made to have speed-detecting*
> *devices fitted to their vehicles.*

As before, this hypothetical evidence seems reasonable. As such, it counts very usefully as evidence.

> *The costs to the National Health Service of young people having so many car*
> *accidents are too high. The NHS is already overstretched having to treat people*
> *suffering from cancer and heart disease. Therefore young people should be made to*
> *have speed-detecting devices fitted to their vehicles.*

This everyday evidence is the sort of thing that you would almost certainly already know. Even so, it is relevant and therefore effective evidence.

PRODUCING TWO REASONS AGAINST THE AUTHOR'S CONCLUSION

So far we have produced arguments with one reason supported by evidence. We can now produce them with two reasons (again, supported by evidence). In the next version, a second reason has been added to the one that we already used.

> *Fitting speed-detecting devices to vehicles will be expensive, a cost that will be*

passed on to all motorists. If the cost is really high, then some motorists could decide not to insure their vehicles.

Not all young drivers break the speed limit more than other drivers.

Therefore young people should not be made to have speed-detecting devices fitted to their vehicles.

This is a useful second reason. The author certainly hasn't considered this, and it does lend support to the opposing conclusion. We can now add some evidence to the reason.

Not all young drivers break the speed limit more than other drivers. If only twenty per cent of young drivers regularly break the speed limit, then most do not need speed-detecting devices fitted to their vehicles.

This hypothetical evidence is not unreasonable. It is very likely that a significant percentage of young drivers drive safely (or, at least, as safely as older drivers). This hypothetical evidence shows the value of such evidence. It stops you from fretting that you don't know an exact figure (percentage, number, rate, and so on). Hypothetical evidence also enables you to be creative. (As long, of course, as the hypothetical evidence isn't unbelievable.)

If you want to use everyday evidence with our second reason, we could try the following.

Not all young drivers break the speed limit more than other drivers. Being caught breaking the speed limit too many times means you get banned from driving, and most young drivers aren't banned from driving.

This might seem a bit thin as evidence, but it's still evidence. It's a sort of observation of what we see around us every day. (You could be critical of the evidence, and say that, even though most young drivers aren't banned from driving, perhaps a relatively higher proportion of them are compared to other age-groups. But, in this exercise, that's not our job.)

Putting our argument together, we have got four versions (two reasons, each with two different types of evidence). Here's one version.

Fitting speed-detecting devices to vehicles will be expensive, a cost that will be passed on to all motorists. If the cost is really high, then some motorists could decide not to insure their vehicles. Not all young drivers break the speed limit more than other drivers. Being caught breaking the speed limit too many times means you get banned from driving, and most young drivers aren't banned from driving. Therefore young people should not be made to have speed-detecting devices fitted to their vehicles.

Just by building up our argument in this way we've created a reasonable argument in which the conclusion isn't really overdrawn.

PRODUCING TWO REASONS FOR THE AUTHOR'S CONCLUSION

We'll now add a second reason to our argument supporting the author's conclusion. So far we've got this (without the supporting evidence included).

The costs to the National Health Service of young people having so many car accidents are too high. Therefore young people should be made to have speed-detecting devices fitted to their vehicles.

We need a second reason that is not something that the author has already used. The following fits that requirement.

Speed-detecting devices could help young inexperienced drivers to develop a greater awareness of the importance of controlling their speed.

This reason fits well with the author's conclusion and gives a new line of argument. We can now add some evidence to support it. We'll provide some hypothetical evidence first.

Speed-detecting devices would help young inexperienced drivers to develop a greater awareness of the importance of controlling their speed. If they drive a modern car, then they won't always be aware of how fast they're actually driving.

This hypothetical evidence lends support to the reason by showing why a speed-detecting device could help young drivers have a greater awareness of the problem of speed. Even if very few young drivers drive modern cars, the evidence – being hypothetical and not being unreasonable – is entirely acceptable.

We now need to consider some everyday evidence.

Speed-detecting devices would help young inexperienced drivers to develop a greater awareness of the importance of controlling their speed. Most driving lessons are spent manoeuvring the car in busy town or city streets, and the instructor won't allow the learner driver to go too fast in them.

This piece of evidence is very much an example of everyday evidence. Even if you haven't yet learned to drive, you will have seen driving school cars being driven around town or city streets, having to go fairly slowly. Everyday it might be, but it still provides some support for the second reason.

We can, as with the argument against the author's conclusion, put together a version of our argument that we have created in support of this conclusion.

The costs to the National Health Service of young people having so many car accidents are too high. The NHS is already overstretched having to treat people suffering from cancer and heart disease. Speed-detecting devices would help young inexperienced drivers to develop a greater awareness of the importance of controlling their speed. If they drive a modern car, then they won't always be aware of how fast they're actually driving. Therefore young people should be made to have speed-detecting devices fitted to their vehicles.

DRAWING INTERMEDIATE CONCLUSIONS

So far, we have constructed various arguments which either supported or opposed the author's conclusion that 'young people should be made to have speed-detecting devices fitted to their cars'.

If we want to develop the arguments even more, we could look at producing more than two reasons. But it is unlikely that you would have to develop them further in this way. It would be seen that, if you can produce two relevant reasons supported by similarly relevant evidence, then you know what you're doing, so you could produce three or more. (Note the hypothetical reasoning there.)

A more likely way that you will be asked to develop an argument further is to provide an intermediate conclusion. We spent some time looking at these in the section on reasons and conclusions. You will remember that intermediate conclusions are drawn on the way to drawing the main conclusion. They can be drawn from only one reason or from more than one. You will also remember the point that intermediate conclusions can be seen as, in a way, finishing an argument, just as any conclusion does. They finish that part of the argument, before it heads off via whatever route to the main conclusion.

We'll now take two of the arguments we have created so far and see how we can draw intermediate conclusions within them. The first is one of the arguments we created against the author's conclusion.

> *Fitting speed-detecting devices to vehicles will be expensive, a cost that will be passed on to all motorists. If the cost is really high, then some motorists could decide not to insure their vehicles. Not all young drivers break the speed limit more than other drivers. Being caught breaking the speed limit too many times means you get banned from driving, and most young drivers aren't banned from driving.*

As we have just considered, an intermediate conclusion is one that can be drawn from either one reason only or from more than one. We'll do it with one reason at first, then go on to draw an intermediate conclusion with both of them.

The second reason is that 'not all young drivers break the speed limit more than other drivers'. We could draw an intermediate conclusion from this.

> *It is wrong to adopt a policy that treats young drivers all the same.*

This might seem a rather big conclusion to draw from this reason, but it would fit with the thrust of this reason. This is that, if not all young drivers speed more than other drivers, it is wrong to treat them as if they do. This intermediate conclusion fits well with the main conclusion that is drawn, in that it supports the argument that we shouldn't fit speed-detecting devices into all young people's vehicles.

If we put it all together, we can see how it fits well.

> *Fitting speed-detecting devices to vehicles will be expensive, a cost that will be passed on to all motorists. If the cost is really high, then some motorists could decide not to insure their vehicles. Not all young drivers break the speed limit more than other drivers. Being caught breaking the speed limit too many times means you get banned from driving, and most young drivers aren't banned from driving. It is wrong to adopt a policy that treats young drivers all the same. Therefore young people should not be made to have speed-detecting devices fitted to their vehicles.*

The structure of the argument is clear.

We can now look at how we could draw an intermediate conclusion from both reasons. To be clear, let's separate them from the rest of the material that we've created.

> *R1: Fitting speed-detecting devices to vehicles will be expensive, a cost that will be passed on to all motorists.*

> *R2: Not all young drivers break the speed limit more than other drivers.*

As you can possibly see, the two reasons together have the force of seeing speed-detecting devices as an unnecessary addition to the cost of insurance. (The point that they're unnecessary comes from the second reason.) So an intermediate conclusion is being strongly hinted at. We can put it in the following way:

> *Putting speed-detecting devices in young people's cars would be an unnecessary addition to the cost of insurance.*

This would lead very effectively to the conclusion that young people shouldn't be made to have these devices in their cars.

Again, we can put the argument back together to see how it fits well.

> *Fitting speed-detecting devices to vehicles will be expensive, a cost that will be passed on to all motorists. If the cost is really high, then some motorists could decide not to insure their vehicles. Not all young drivers break the speed limit more than other drivers. Being caught breaking the speed limit too many times means you get banned from driving, and most young drivers aren't banned from driving. Putting speed-detecting devices in young people's cars would be an unnecessary addition to the cost of insurance. Therefore young people should not be made to have speed-detecting devices fitted to their vehicles.*

Just to complete things, we can add an intermediate conclusion to our argument in support of the author's conclusion. This is one of the versions that we created.

> *The costs to the National Health Service of young people having so many car accidents are too high. The NHS is already overstretched having to treat people suffering from cancer and heart disease. Speed-detecting devices would help young inexperienced drivers to develop a greater awareness of the importance of controlling their speed. If they drive a modern car, then they won't always be aware of how fast they're actually driving. Therefore young people should be made to have speed-detecting devices fitted to their vehicles.*

We'll draw an intermediate conclusion this time from the first reason. This reason uses the words 'too high' when describing the costs to the NHS of young people having car accidents. This gives us a useful route to take in drawing an intermediate conclusion. If the costs are 'too high', then we can conclude that:

We need to reduce the risk of young people having car accidents.

As we have reminded ourselves earlier, an intermediate conclusion completes an argument (within a wider argument). If we add this intermediate conclusion to the first reason we get the following:

The costs to the National Health Service of young people having so many car accidents are too high. Therefore we need to reduce the risk of young people having car accidents.

This produces a short but complete argument. The conclusion fits well with the reason, such that it is not overdrawn. But we'll put it all back together to see how the intermediate conclusion works as support for the main conclusion.

The costs to the National Health Service of young people having so many car accidents are too high. The NHS is already overstretched having to treat people suffering from cancer and heart disease. Therefore we need to reduce the risk of young people having car accidents. Speed-detecting devices would help young inexperienced drivers to develop a greater awareness of the importance of controlling their speed. If they drive a modern car, then they won't always be aware of how fast they're actually driving. Therefore young people should be made to have speed-detecting devices fitted to their vehicles.

INCLUDING COUNTER-ARGUMENTS

We have already considered counter-arguments or counter-claims when we were looking at special kinds of argument content. In producing your own arguments, you might want (or be asked) to include a counter-argument or counter-claim/assertion. We'll use our argument against the author's conclusion to see how we might do this.

Remember that a counter-position in an argument is normally there in order to be knocked down. So a good place to put it is at the beginning, such that your argument then does the knocking down.

Since the author is arguing that young people should have speed-detecting devices fitted to their cars, a counter-position has to set up a claim that suggests that such a thing would not be a good thing.

> *It is often argued that we should always put people's right to privacy above most other things.*

This claim, as you can see, fits very uncomfortably with the author's recommendation that we put devices in young people's cars in order to allow insurance companies to monitor their driving at all times. To emphasise how this contrasts with the argument that we've produced in support of the author's argument, we'll change the order of the reasons (there's no significance to the order: a reason is a reason, wherever it is). (We've also changed the second 'therefore' into a 'so' to make that part of the argument read less clumsily.)

> *It is often argued that we should always put people's right to privacy above most other things. However, speed-detecting devices would help young inexperienced drivers to develop a greater awareness of the importance of controlling their speed. If they drive a modern car, then they won't always be aware of how fast they're actually driving. The costs to the National Health Service of young people having so many car accidents are too high. The NHS is already overstretched having to treat people suffering from cancer and heart disease. Therefore we need to reduce the risk of young people having car accidents. So young people should be made to have speed-detecting devices fitted to their vehicles.*

You will have seen the introduction of the word 'however' at the beginning of the second sentence. Hopefully, you will remember that, when we looked at counter-positions, we looked at how authors normally use a word like this to indicate that their argument was about to begin.

If we were to look back at our argument against the author's position, we can see that we could put in a counter-position in the same way. This has to be a version of an argument that sees the value in controlling drivers' speeding in some way.

> *Since speed is one of the main causes of accidents, insurance companies argue that, in the interests of all motorists, they must tackle the problem by installing speed-detecting devices in young people's vehicles.*

This presents a counter-argument, with a reason 'speed is one of the main causes of accidents' and a conclusion 'in the interests of all motorists, insurance companies must tackle the problem by installing speed-detecting devices in young people's vehicles.' Our argument will respond to this, as below.

Since speed is one of the main causes of accidents, insurance companies argue that, in the interests of all motorists, they must tackle the problem by installing speed-detecting devices in young people's vehicles. But, fitting speed-detecting devices to vehicles will be expensive, a cost that will be passed on to all motorists. If the cost is really high, then some motorists could decide not to insure their vehicles. Not all young drivers break the speed limit more than other drivers. Being caught breaking the speed limit too many times means you get banned from driving, and most young drivers aren't banned from driving. Putting speed-detecting devices in young people's cars would be an unnecessary addition to the cost of insurance. Therefore young people should not be made to have speed-detecting devices fitted to their vehicles.

Again, then, we have created an argument that contains a counter-argument, two reasons (each with supporting evidence), an intermediate conclusion, and a main conclusion. If you look at it now, it looks impressive, but remember that it was produced by building it up bit by bit, section by section. Producing an argument is best seen in terms of the assembling of bits, just like a wall starts off life as a pile of bricks.

So, continuing with the analogy, if you've got this far, you can build a house. Well done.

If you want to know how ... to learn the skills of critical assessment and effective argument

'Much attention is now given to the subject of 'thinking skills' or 'core skills'. The idea behind this emphasis on such skills is that, whatever the specific subject you are studying, you are going to be using skills common to many subjects. So, if you can develop and improve these skills, then your performance in the subjects you are studying should also be developed and improved.'

Roy van den Brink-Budgen

Critical Thinking for Students
Learn the skills of critical assessment and effective argument
Roy van den Brink-Budgen

Critical Thinking is a core skill needed to make all your studies more effective. This totally revised and updated book is a must if you want to find out how to develop your own arguments and evaluate other people's.

'When teaching for the OCR AS-level course I found this an ideal book – the right depth for teachers and the right length for students. It is written with such obvious enthusiasm for lucid and practical thinking that it can be recommended to teachers and students in any field.' – *Roger Sutcliffe, President, Sapere*

ISBN 1 85703 634 4

If you want to know how ... to pass exams every time

'Exam success isn't only for the clever and hard working. Success comes as much, if not more, from your attitude to exams, the way you approach the course of study and some simple techniques to use on the day itself.

'A universal culture of fear, worry and stress has developed around exams. But it really needn't be like this for you. In this book I will dispel the common myths surrounding exams and show you how to adopt a positive and confident approach.'
Mike Evans

How to Pass Exams Every Time
Proven techniques for any exam that will boost your confidence and guarantee success
Mike Evans

Reading this book really will make a huge difference to exam performance, whatever exams you're taking. It isn't just hard work and intelligence that gets you through. In fact many hard working, intelligent people fail through lack of confidence or poor exam technique. At least 50 per cent of your chances are down to: your attitude to exams; the way you approach the course of study; and simple but effective techniques to use in the exam itself. These techniques are your guarantee of success – and what's more they're easy to learn and proven beyond doubt!

'Brisk, shrewd and full of useful tips.' – *Daily Telegraph*

ISBN 1 85703 933 5

If you want to know how … to write an essay

'This book will be of benefit to students at any age from 14 to MA level. I believe that those students who begin to use it at 14 will still be benefiting from it in any tertiary courses they take up. I have outlined the principles and shown them in action in as simple and direct a manner as possible. The essential advice doesn't change from one level to the other: the quality and depth of the essay required at different stages will be forthcoming if the skills have been developed and the knowledge obtained.'
Brendan Hennessy

Writing an Essay
Simple techniques to transform your coursework and examinations
Brendan Hennessy

This lively and practical guide takes you through the whole process. With it you'll write essays of distinction every time.

'There's a lot of good sense in this book.' – *Times Educational Supplement*

'If you're a student, buy it.' – *Writer's Monthly*

1 85703 846 0

How To Books are available through all good bookshops, or you can order direct from us through Grantham Book Services.

Tel: +44 (0)1476 541080
Fax: +44 (0)1476 541061
Email: orders@gbs.tbs-ltd.co.uk

Or via our website
www.howtobooks.co.uk

To order via any of these methods please quote the title(s) of the book(s) and your credit card number together with its expiry date.

For further information about our books and catalogue, please contact:

How To Books
3 Newtec Place
Magdalen Road
Oxford OX4 1RE

Visit our web site at
www.howtobooks.co.uk

Or you can contact us by email at info@howtobooks.co.uk